Living the
LITTLE OFFICE

Living the LITTLE OFFICE

Reflections on the Little Office of the Blessed Virgin Mary

Sister Marianna Gildea, R.S.M.

COLLEGE MISERICORDIA
DALLAS, PENNSYLVANIA

ANGELUS PRESS
2915 FOREST AVENUE
KANSAS CITY, MISSOURI 64109

Nihil Obstat
Thomas J. McHugh, LL.D.
Censor Librorum

Imprimatur
Henry T. Klonowski, D.D.
Administrator,
Diocese of Scranton

July 4, 1954

Originally published by College Misericordia. Second printing
August, 1955.

ANGELUS PRESS

2915 FOREST AVENUE
KANSAS CITY, MISSOURI 64109
PHONE (816) 753-3150
FAX (816) 753-3557
ORDER LINE 1-800-966-7337
www.angeluspress.org

ISBN 978-1-892331-81-6
FIRST PRINTING–July 2010

Printed in the United States of America

To

MARY

MOTHER OF MERCY

AND

QUEEN OF HEAVEN

FOREWORD

$\mathcal{T}$HE beauty and richness of THE LITTLE OFFICE OF THE BLESSED VIRGIN is not unknown to those who recite it daily. Yet the day by day routine, with its many distractions and demands, sometimes may make it somewhat of a burden, even for the most fervent religious. Sister Marianna's book will not provide the perfect solution. No book can. But to those who are seeking to raise their recitation from mere routine to fervent worship of God and praise of Mary, this book will help. And it will help largely because the meditations and reflections are written by a person who knows what it is to be busy. As a Professor of Romance Languages in one of our finest Catholic colleges for women, her life is consecrated to God not only through the hours spent in the classroom but through the many other activities that follow a teaching Sister wherever she goes. It is evident that the inspiration that produced this book comes from one who is living the life of Martha, but who wants to be Mary.

Sisters from the many religious communities whose Rule calls for the daily recitation of THE LITTLE OFFICE will be grateful for this work. Perhaps, too, it will reach many of our lay people who would like to recite THE LITTLE OFFICE but who need a guide to its treasures. May the Holy Spirit lead many to the pages of this book, that through its gentle guidance they may find ever better ways of *Living The Little Office*.

Reverend George S. DePrizio, C.S.C.

January 21, 1955.

PREFACE

For a good many years I have been searching for a series of meditations which might benefit the average religious in the recitation of THE LITTLE OFFICE OF THE BLESSED VIRGIN MARY. While the current interest in the liturgical movement has resulted in many excellent publications, throwing light on the obscurity of the Psalms, these scholarly works are not always of practical value to those who have very little time or opportunity for the examination of critical studies on the subject.

The purpose of this volume, therefore, is to present some practical reflections on the liturgical prayers of THE LITTLE OFFICE. It is intended principally for beginners, since it attempts to show those unfamiliar with THE LITTLE OFFICE how perfectly its prayers apply to present needs. It seeks to call attention to the inexhaustible treasure of spiritual beauty remaining comparatively unexplored by those whose many duties require them to recite THE OFFICE hurriedly every day. It endeavors to prove that the inspired wisdom of Holy Scripture can develop a deep absorption in prayer, needed to balance the scientific industry of our atomic age. It urges the contemplation of the wonders of God's creation by laymen, rubbing elbows with a busy world.

Consequently, this little study does not claim to be exhaustive, but merely suggestive. It is for those who consecrate their lives to the Lord amidst the burdens of strenuous labor. It is for those engaged in active works of mercy who seek union with God, through simple, liturgical prayer. It is for those who seek identification with Christ in a life of prayer, love, and sacrifice, as they generously spend their lives in the interests of social welfare. It is especially for those who wish to serve the Lord through Mary, the Queen of Heaven.

While the reactions to these Psalm verses are naturally those of a Sister of an active community of religious, they may interest all members of the lay apostolate. Devout laymen, as well as religious, can always find the reading of the Psalms of THE LITTLE OFFICE a means of improving the quality of their prayer. If, through the mysterious operation of God's grace, these reflections should encourage even one soul to seek a deeper knowledge of Sacred Scripture or the liturgy, so that this soul may love and praise God better through Mary in her LITTLE OFFICE, this volume can become a modest supplement to the numerous fruitful achievements of the Marian Year.

The preference of the average religious for concentrating on subjects of meditation taken from the New Testament is certainly admirable, but this appreciation for the life of our divine Lord will become more profound through a study of the long advent prior to His Nativity. Thus, something of the totality of the redemptive plan can be better perceived from the serious consideration of the inspired writings which reveal the ardent and solid faith of those longing for a Redeemer.

The very organization of the liturgy obviously illustrates this intention of Holy Mother Church. In the Holy Sacrifice of the Mass, the center of religious worship, the spotlight is focused on the life and teachings of our Lord, culminating in the drama of Calvary, a perpetuation of the divine and perfect oblation. THE OFFICE, largely dependent on Old Testament sources, furnishes a more extensive preparation and thanksgiving for this sublime event. It thus provides an excellent opportunity to those who recite it daily, especially religious, to increase their fervent preparation and thanksgiving for the Holy Sacrifice.

To the novice, or lay apostle, the Psalms, lessons, and antiphons appear very obscure and rather remote from the duties of an active life. Usually, the training for the proper recitation of THE OFFICE in choir confines itself to the perfection of its oral rendition and its rubrics. Without some aid concerning the genuine significance of its content, this magnificent part of the liturgy leaves the intelligent Catholic often groping along, only occasionally aware, and then quite vaguely, of the radiant splendor to be glimpsed by one in his position. Gradually, his advanced studies may make him more keenly aware of the spiritual value and beauty of THE OFFICE. Too frequently even the religious becomes immersed in such a multiplicity of activities that this prayer becomes a real burden in his daily round of duties. Probably this is less likely to happen with theologians versed in the study of Sacred Scripture. But because religious women who recite THE LITTLE OFFICE usually have little opportunity for this type of education, they would seem to have greater need for developing their knowledge of the Old Testament where, incidentally, arise such noble examples of valiant women.

Because the present work offers individual reflections suggested by the Scriptural texts, these ideas are recorded verse by verse. It follows the critical edition of the Psalter recently published in Latin by the professors of the Pontifical Biblical Institute. The English translation is that copyrighted by the Confraternity of Christian Doctrine. Where Scriptural references occur within the reflections proper, they usually follow the Douay version of the Bible.

The suggestions arising from the Psalm verses are, for the most part, necessarily brief. Certainly, as one moves rapidly through the recitation of THE OFFICE in choir, there is not much leisure for meditative thinking. These reflections are presented simply to show how each thought expressed in THE OFFICE may be taken separately as a profitable subject for meditation. By no means is it proposed that one should linger at every verse during the recitation of the several Hours! The soul may delight in this spiritual luxury only when it rises to the celestial choirs in the contemplation of eternal Truth.

The plan followed here is simply the order of the liturgical prayers of THE LITTLE OFFICE OF THE BLESSED VIRGIN MARY, from the preparatory prayer to the concluding *Sacrosanctae*. First, the beginning of the ecclesiastical year is considered in the *Matins* and

Lauds of the Advent cycle; next, appear the Little Hours of the Christmas season; and finally, the *Vespers* and *Compline* of the ordinary OFFICE, ending with the triumphant hymn, *Regina coeli,* proper to the feast of the Resurrection. In order not to distract the reader by interrupting the single sequence of *Matins,* the variant nocturns, the lessons common to seasons outside Advent, and the *Te Deum* have been placed at the end of *Matins.*

As a leitmotif, running through the liturgical expressions of praise of the Lord, we find the antiphons[1] in honor of our Blessed Mother. To the uninitiated, these insertions may appear as inconsistent digressions, destructive of the logical unity of THE OFFICE. Not so, to the devout worshipper. His mood is aptly described by Dante, as he pictures for us Saint Anne in Paradise:

> Over against Peter see Anna sit, so satisfied to gaze upon her daughter that she removeth not her eyes to sing Hosanna.   (*Par.* 32: 133)

This does not mean any neglect of the Lord or irreverence towards Him. It merely signifies that, as we rejoice in praising the Lord, we rejoice also in the perfection of the one representative of our humanity elected to be His mother. Amidst our reflections suggested by the Psalms of the Old Testament, we glance at her who was prophesied as the new Eve who would come to crush the serpent's head. We look to her for inspiration and example in the simple and true adoration of God.

Less attention has been given to the analysis and study of the hymns than to the Psalms of THE OFFICE, for two reasons: first, the later compositions, although expressive of profound truths, are not likely to be so obscure, and therefore, they do not require so much elaborate commentary as do the ancient hymns; furthermore, the medieval hymns can be much more thoroughly appreciated in other readily available references, particularly that of Father Britt[2]. Any attempt to render more intelligible their excellent translations seems unnecessary. However, in order not to break the continuity of THE OFFICE, I have applied the method of paraphrasing to some of these admirable hymns; to the stanzas of others, I have merely applied captions, as if one were contemplating the titles for a triptych. The obvious significance of the prayers at the end of the several Hours eliminated the necessity for further comment.

The point of view is admittedly modern. It results from an attempt to see in the Psalms some application and expression of our own religious sentiments and convictions. Consequently, in the Messianic Psalms, for example, we consider the prophecies and yearnings of the Psalmist as fulfilled rather than to be fulfilled. This deliberate telescoping of time and space is intended to help us see in the trials and tribulations of the Hebrews and their remarkable expressions of faith, a mirror of our own troubled times. It allows us to view the relations between God and man in the light of their eternal significance.

---

1 Cf. Pius Parsch, *The Breviary Explained* (St. Louis, Herder, 1952), pp. 123, f.

2 *Hymns of the Breviary and Missal* (New York, Benziger, 1948).

Here, I must express appreciation to the Episcopal Committee for permission to use, as the basic text for these reflections, the English translation of the Psalms and Canticles copyrighted by the Confraternity of Christian Doctrine. My sincere acknowledgment is due also to Frederick Pustet Company, to Benziger Brothers, and to the Oxford University Press, for allowing the use of material taken from their publications. Deserving grateful recognition for particular favors are: Miss Miriam Marks, executive secretary of the Confraternity of Christian Doctrine, at the National Center; Mr. Eugene J. Butler, head of the Legal Department of the National Catholic Welfare Conference; Messrs. Thomas J. Collins, Sr. and Jr., of the Collins Press; and Mr. James A. McKane, of the Square Printing Company.

Since these reflections have developed over a long period of years, originally with a view to spiritual profit rather than scholarly documentation, it is impossible to give due credit to their precise, individual sources.

In a special way, I wish to thank religious superiors for their genuine interest in the project and their kindly encouragement. For the critical review of the manuscript and for numerous helpful suggestions, I am very grateful to the Right Reverend John J. Sheerin, Protonotary Apostolic and Vicar General of the Diocese of Paterson, New Jersey. For his wise counsel and careful supervision of the work, I am deeply indebted, likewise, to Reverend George S. DePrizio, C.S.C., Dean of King's College, Wilkes-Barre, Pennsylvania.

To many other friends, to relatives, particularly to Sister Mary Davidica, R.S.M., and to all the other Sisters who contributed in any way to the production of *Living the Little Office*, I am most grateful. As we sing our hymns of praise, let us pray fervently for all these "good neighbors" whose love of the Lord is evidenced by their practical charity.

Sister Marianna, R.S.M.

"...*The most pressing duty of Christians, is to live the liturgical life, and increase and cherish its supernatural spirit.*"

—Encyclical Letter of Pope Pius XII on the Sacred Liturgy, *Mediator Dei.*

APERI, DOMINE

$\mathcal{T}$HE day has been long
and we are weary . . . cooking . . . nursing . . . teaching . . .
perhaps giving catechetical instruction after regular class hours.
Reverently, we proceed into Your tabernacled Presence, Lord
. . . and breathe a quiet sigh of relief as we slip into our
accustomed place. We know the sacred privilege of joining
with the angels in offering praise to Your divine Majesty, but
our minds are on ourselves and on how much we are doing.
Fatigue dulls our consciousness, at least temporarily, during
this act of worship. Routine tends to make us concentrate on
our petty troubles rather than on the one thing alone necessary.
We keep wondering about that disciplinary problem presented
by irrepressible little Tommy . . . or about that patient in 202
. . . or what to have for the approaching feast day dinner . . . or
whether the pastor will agree to that special project . . . or how
we could change the arrangement of flowers on the altar . . .
or how this month's bills can possibly be paid.

Interrupting this jangled series of perplexing reflections,
come the tolls announcing the OFFICE of *Matins* and *Lauds*.
Mechanically, the choir manual is opened as the Superior in-
tones, *Aperi, Domine*.

*O*PEN *my mouth, O Lord* . . .

The rest of the prayer is said silently, intimately· dear Lord, open my mouth . . . the mouth which has begun the day with Your praise . . . the mouth whose first utterance this morning was the offering to You of all my prayers, works, sufferings, and joys . . . the mouth so eager to shelter Your Sacramental Self at Holy Mass.

To bless Your holy Name . . .

To recognize You as Creator and to praise You is the most noble act in which a creature can engage. Thus rendering extrinsic glory to God are the angels unceasingly occupied. Thus the saints spend their eternity.

Members of the most holy Trinity, Father, Son, and Holy Ghost . . . You are omniscient . . . You each clearly perceive the absolute perfection found in Yourselves and in each other . . . You alone are capable of rendering intrinsic glory to Your divine Essence. The clearer the knowledge, the greater is the possibility of praise. Since You alone, O God, possess infinite knowledge, You alone can render to Yourself the infinite glory proper to Your divine nature. But You allow us, Your children, to glorify You in our own limited and imperfect manner. Indeed, the primary purpose for which we have been created is for Your extrinsic glory. We can contribute to this extrinsic glory by increasing our knowledge of You and by participating in Your praise. According to the degree of our intelligence of spiritual matters, we may thus render You great glory here on earth, if we try, by utilizing to advantage the gifts of Your Holy Spirit.

Cleanse my heart also from all vain, perverse, and distracting thoughts . . .

Yes, Lord, cleanse my heart from all these vain, silly, stupid, and trivial inanities which keep me from listening to Your abiding voice in my heart. Keep me also from all other thoughts which feed foolish self-love and distract me from my one single, steady purpose of honoring You always and above all things.

Enlighten my understanding, inflame my affections . . .

I recall, of course, the three ways of reciting worthily THE OFFICE: by saying the words attentively and accurately . . . by saying the words while pondering on their meaning . . . by saying the words with affection and devotion, desiring to please You and praise You, O Lord, whether or not I comprehend the meaning of the words. Help me, then, in these days of maximum efficiency and super-production, to praise You with the maximum degree of spiritual energy, grace, and power! Let not my words descend to the level of cold, mechanical, motor activity . . . but enlighten my intellect, that it may delight in the penetration and contemplation of Your Word. Inflame my heart, that it may be inspired to noble love and heroic sacrifice.

So that worthily . . . according to my capacity . . . in a serious, solemn, and becoming manner . . . *attentively and devoutly . . . I may recite this* OFFICE.

And may I deserve to be heard in the sight of Your divine Majesty.

Help me to realize that Your eyes are upon me, as I attempt to offer this prayer.

Through Christ, our Lord.

Through the infinite perfection of Your Son, O Lord, may my gross imperfections and awkward blunderings be transformed into offerings pleasing to You.

Amen. So be it . . . This is my earnest desire.

O Lord, I offer these hours to You, in union with that divine intention with which You offered praises to God, while You were on earth.

May I be ever conscious of this intention expressed by You, that I must "be about my Father's business" (Luke 2: 49).

II

MATINS

Hail Mary, full of grace!

Help me to perform this privileged function of participating in the Lord's praises with all possible energy and spiritual vigor. Since the value of praise is usually increased in accordance with the worth of the individual uttering it, pray, O Mediatrix of all graces, so richly endowed and such a perfect instrument of the most High! Pray that I may increase daily in grace ... not merely for my own spiritual benefit, but primarily for God's glory and for the manifold blessings that such prayer may bring down on corporate Christianity ... on the members of the Mystical Body of Christ on earth ... on the suffering souls who long for release from their bonds.

The Lord is with thee ...

O Mary, full of grace, help me, dear Lady, whose help has never been sought in vain.

Blessed art thou amongst women ...

O model of all religious! Lead us religious women, under the mantle of your mercy, to be ardent members in the choir of divine praise, as well as efficient instruments of divine mercy.

And blessed is the fruit of thy womb, Jesus!

As Spouses of Christ, may we be increasingly fruitful in the highest prayer and most noble works of charity ... that we may engender a greater knowledge and love of our Lord in all those whom we influence ... directly, in our active duties ... or indirectly, through intercessory prayer.

Holy Mary, Mother of God!

Holy Mary, Mother of God and our Mother, guide us in the way of holiness, by teaching us a ready submission and resignation to the divine Will ... according to the duties ordained and assigned. Teach us to avoid ambitious striving and idle dreaming. Teach us to realize that our Lord has His special plan for each of His children ... the plan on which our sanctification and salvation depend.

Pray for us sinners ...

Pray for us, since we fail so many times in our rebellious, cross-grained natures, to see the hand of Providence in our affairs ... because our spiritual immaturity obscures our vision and makes us very stubborn children indeed. Pray *now* ... that we be not estranged from God. Pray *always* ... that we may persevere and profit by every grace-*ful* opportunity to praise, love, reverence, serve, and adore His Majesty. Pray especially for us in that dread hour when all hell let loose will engage in one last, mighty offensive to wrest our souls from our Creator's power ... in that fatal and irrevocable *hour of our death.* Pray that in our physical weakness we may be spiritually strong ... endowed with the divine armour of virtue ... that we may not succumb to the wiles and snares ... the lies, the false assurances, the mines, the booby traps, the hidden explosives calculated to insure our defeat ... but that we will struggle with vigilance, courage, and heroism, until we conquer and find at last peace ... an everlasting peace, guaranteed by the protection and happiness of our heavenly home. *Amen.*

$\mathcal{T}$HOU, *O Lord, wilt open my lips.*

Open these lips, O Lord, which have instructed Your children ... comforted Your suffering ... consoled and encouraged Your friends today. Dear Lord, if these lips have uttered anything this day unworthy of a Spouse of Christ, help these words of praise about to be spoken, nullify, diminish, or, by Your redemptive grace, repair the evil they have done!

And my tongue shall announce Thy praise.

With Your blessing thus placed upon my lips, Lord, Who cleansed the lips of Your prophet Isaias with a burning coal, I can proceed to use my mouth for the most noble purpose for which it was created, not simply as a channel for the admission of bodily food ... but as an instrument of the spirit, as a medium of worship. How admirable is this articulate power ... a bridge which spans the abyss between spirit and spirit ... a bridge over which may pass knowledge and desires, garbed in the semblance of sounds! O supreme Pontifex, Who bridged the abyss between earth and heaven, grant that this delicate vocal instrument of mine be well guarded ... that the ideas and wishes transmitted to others may be such as will be for their spiritual edification and profit. O supreme Pontifex, Who, through the gift of faith, bridges the infinite abyss between creature and Creator, make me articulate in divine praise ... to express what divine Light makes my mind know of You ... to declare what divine Love makes my heart feel for You!

Incline unto my aid, O God.

Conscious, O God, that You alone are capable of rendering adequate praise and honor to Your infinite perfections, we are overwhelmed with awesome fear at our own temerity ... rushing in where angels and saints can only bow in profound adoration! Yes, Lord, we would certainly hesitate to participate in this liturgical act ... to chant the LITTLE OFFICE OF THE BLESSED VIRGIN MARY, since we feel the weight of our unworthiness. Nevertheless, the thought of Holy Mass gives us courage. There in this central act of liturgical worship, Holy Mother Church has us pray, "that ... we may be made partakers of His divinity Who vouchsafed to become partaker of our humanity ..." (Offertory prayer). Furthermore, in the Holy Sacrifice, our divine Lord Jesus Christ, Your Son, immolates Himself to You, O Father ... thus rendering in our behalf infinite adoration, as well as reparation for our offences, supplication for new favors, and thanksgiving for benefits already received. This thought renews our courage for reciting THE OFFICE. Hence, still over-awed, but confident ... feeling all the misery of our littleness we cry:

O Lord, make haste to help me.

O Lord, Jesus Christ, hasten to help us praise the other members of the blessed Trinity! Our Father, Who will not refuse Your children, please help us honor Your beloved Son and the Holy Spirit of Love uniting Him with You. O sanctifying Spirit, assist us in the adoration of our heavenly Father and His only begotten Son! Amidst the glorious exchange of praises of Father, Son, and Holy Ghost, we prostrate ourselves in spirit, filled with wondrous awe and admiration that somehow. even the most feeble expression of prayer and praise,

uttered in the most awkward fashion by the lowliest of creatures, can be elevated, sanctified, and divinized, thus contribu-
ting to Your greater glory, O God! We contemplate once more
the blessings won for us by You, O divine Redeemer, as we
recall the prayer of the Minor Elevation at Holy Mass:
"Through Him, and with Him, and in Him, be unto Thee, O
God the Father almighty, in the unity of the Holy Ghost, all
honor and glory, world without end."

Glory be to the Father, and to the Son, and to the Holy Ghost.

My limited knowledge would necessarily limit the adequacy
of my love and praise . . . but faith and hope in You, O members of the most holy Trinity . . . charity magnified by Your
infinite power . . . will elevate my prayers, divinize them . . .
and transform them into something of supernatural worth!
Thus am I privileged to draw from the depths of Your riches
and wisdom and knowledge, my God (Cf. Romans 11: 33).
O profound mystery! O ineffable and infinite treasure, which
I lavishly spend in each *Gloria!*

*As it was in the beginning, is now, and ever shall be, world
without end. Amen.*

As it was in the beginning . . . is now . . . and ever shall be . . .
this means eternally. Yes, Lord, let my praise be not limited
in power nor even in time. I would wish to praise You not just
now . . . I regret not having spent every minute of my whole
life engaged exclusively in performing this glorious act. Too
little, too *lackadaisically,* have I loved You, if not with Saint
Augustine, too *late.* I should like to spend every minute from
now on . . . in just this same manner. The nine choirs of angels
devote themselves entirely to singing Your praises. But I am
not an angel, Lord, nor have I power to make my praise perpetual. Even today I have many things to do, so that my
formal expression of love and worship must soon cease. Of
course, I understand, *laborare est orare.* But sometimes I become over-solicitous about the *minutiae* of my particular labors,
so that I behave as if the active life could be substituted for the
contemplative . . . as if it is even preferable to it! O most holy
Trinity! You are eternal! Dear Father, Son, and Holy Ghost!
According to faith, You reside now within the temple of my
soul. Teach me to reconcile contemplative prayer with active
duties. O Jesus, Who while on earth taught and ministered to
the needs of mankind, yet never ceased to contemplate the face
of Your Father in heaven, please supply for the praise that I
would like now to give . . . that I would like to have given in the

past . . . that I desire earnestly to give in the future. May I ask You thus to make acceptable the praise and prayer that I, Your weak creature, am almost afraid to present? to make infinite my very limited offerings? Thus, this world of time—every moment of it—becomes everlastingly joyous. Help me now and always to spend each moment in faithful devotion to duty and in the consciousness of Your most sacred Presence. As You, O eternal High Priest, solemnly offer to Your Father this glorious prayer of everlasting praise . . . may I, with the other members of Your Mystical Body, whether at labor or at prayer, respond sincerely, humbly, adoringly, *Amen.*

Alleluja. Praise the Lord! May we become more and more conscious of our sublime privilege and duty of offering this prayer of praise.

INVITATORY

*H*AIL *Mary, full of grace, the Lord is with thee.*

O gracious and graceful Lady, Mediatrix of all graces! Pray that we may daily grow in grace . . . cooperate fully with grace . . . and be ever loyal and devoted to the Source of all grace, Who resides now in our souls.

PSALM 94

*C*OME, *let us sing joyfully to the Lord.*

"Come, friends, rejoice we in the Lord's honor."[1] To participate earnestly in the Invitatory Psalm, we must share its communal spirit. Come, friends, let us rejoice in honor of the Lord. Joy is contagious and increases when communicated. Spiritual joy cannot be selfish. O Lord, now the total pattern of Your law of charity requiring love of one's neighbor as proof of love of You becomes crystal clear: if we love You truly, God, we must want everyone else to love You, too. Here we are, singing Your praises with the other members of our religious community. Surely, the genuine happiness shared together of praising You will make us forget our individual peculiarities. Human lovers are blind to each other's failings and disregard their own personal defects because of their joy in sharing blessings and sorrows together. If we really love and praise You, O God, our exultation will make us rejoice in Your perfections in spite of the total sum of our own numerous imperfections.

---

1 Cf. Rev. R. Knox, *Psalms* (New York, Sheed, Ward, 1947), p. 94.

Nor is our joyous love and praise to be restricted to members of our religious community. When we recite THE OFFICE, we are privileged to be representatives of Your Church before Your heavenly throne, O God. Hence, we are praying for all the members of the Mystical Body of Christ. Come, friends in Christ, from near and far! Let us rejoice together in the Lord's honor and let us represent others who would like to join this choir of praise, but cannot . . . because of the burden of other duties . . . or because of physical or spiritual suffering . . . or because they are victims of false and vicious propaganda. Let us praise for those who will not praise . . . for those bent on pleasure . . . on ambitious enterprise . . . on art or science for its own sake . . . on the accumulation of wealth . . . let us praise for those who have very little or no faith.

"Rejoice we in the Lord's honor" . . . and, without the aid of microphone or dials, transformers or power stations, this joyful paean of praise resounds throughout the entire earth . . . is re-echoed in the celestial, sweet and solemn harmonies intoned before supernal Beauty!

Let us acclaim the Rock of our salvation.

"Cry we out merrily to God, our strength and deliverer!"[1] Enthusiastically, we wish to shout with joy and admiration. Of course, the rubrics scarcely allow the uninhibited enthusiasm of the sports' fan who witnesses exciting spectacles in the playing field. The significant solemnity of our worship requires a dignified, if joyful, reverence. Nevertheless, enthusiasm should be the keynote of this Psalm, intense . . . in fact, more intense . . . if well-disciplined by ascetic reserve. Dullness of spirit as a substitute for discipline would rapidly devitalize our prayer. Let us cast off sloth . . . let us praise the Lord ardently, earnestly, vigorously!

Let us greet Him with thanksgiving; let us joyfully sing psalms to Him.

Come, friends . . . this is no ordinary invitation! If you were invited to leave aside business or professional cares and enjoy congenial company on a delightful trip to the mountains in a new Cadillac, you would gladly accept; or, if you were privileged to ascend skyward and enjoy the wondrous realms of the stratosphere, gliding along in the most modern airliner, that would be most exhilarating! But *this* invitation is much more delightful! This invitation will bring you into the spiritual stratosphere of grace . . . into the elite society of angels and

1 Cf. Knox, *op. cit.*

saints...into the very Presence of the most High! Be not
afraid of what to say or how to behave in the court of the Lord.
It will be a formal occasion, my friends, but we shall thoroughly enjoy it! Could we express our joy more properly according
to protocol than by using the inspired word of God, the Psalms,
to acknowledge the happiness of our faith?

Hail, Mary, full of grace, the Lord is with thee. Our Lady,
full of grace, teach us jubilant reverence before the throne of
God!

For the Lord is a great God, and a great King above all gods.

Yes, we are overawed by lords of industry, law, or politics;
masters of engineering or technology; distinguished authors,
journalists; men eminent for their scholarship or professional
skill; financial wizards; scientific geniuses; leaders in every
field. We feel rather uncomfortable and strained in their presence, if indeed the host of vigilant secretaries in their service
ever admit us into their sacrosanct company! But, dear Lord,
You are a great God and a mighty King above all gods. The
so-called great of this world are very insignificant individuals,
infinitesimal in stature and power, compared to You, Who are
truly Lord and Ruler of all things, as well as God of all perfections.

Dear Lord, in contrast to the great of this world...or the
so-called great... You, although infinitely perfect, deign to be
accessible to us always, deign to be near us, desire our frequent
visits, even if these reflect a certain haste, routine, or even in-
attention. This personal concern for us individually...which
caused us to come into being and henceforth to be the object of
so much divine attention...cannot leave us untouched. Keep
us aware always of this love, O Lord, that we may return it
according to our capacity. Deepen that capacity, that our love
for You may increase. No, You will not reject Your people, O
Lord! Creation, Redemption and the remarkable opportunities
for sanctification through prayer and the sacraments prove this.
But do not allow us to reject You, O Lord! Through indifference or timidity, let us not feel that we are consuming with
our petty troubles Your precious time, since time for You is
eternity! Let us realize fully that we are Your people, O Lord,
made children of God by Baptism. Our Father, we have complete confidence in Your paternal care!

In His hands are the depths of the earth . . .

Infinite is Your perfection, O Lord . . . infinite Your love . . .
infinite Your power. Your divine providence rules us and all
our milieu . . . in the sequence of time . . . in the extent of
space. We benefit by Your provident care, from the products
of the remotest limits of earth: coffee, pepper, silk, rubber . . .
to mention only a few. The inventions of science . . . the telephone, the airplane, radio, television, radar . . . reduce space to
a marvelous degree. If human knowledge and energy can effect
such results, what can we not expect of divine knowledge and
power? Swifter than science are the wings of the spirit. Not
only time, but space is telescoped in Eternity . . . in the limitless
Here . . . in the everlasting Now.

and the tops of the mountains are His.

From an airplane, mountains do not look so formidable as
they do when one attempts to climb them. From the vantage
point of eternity, O God, You see the entire pattern of our lives
. . . present, past, and future. You Who rule beyond the heights
of mountains are aware of all obstacles, great and small, our
ups and downs of life which succeed each other. Your all-wise
providence sees every turn in the road of our lives and bestows
on us the grace to travel this road wisely . . . helping our neighbor as we go. Perfect trust in You, our all-wise and loving
Father, humble resignation to Your divine plan, will be the
most sincere tribute of praise we can offer. Hail, Mary, full of
grace! When mountainous perplexities loom on our horizon,
teach us to say: "Be it done to me according to Thy word"
(Luke 1: 38).

The Lord is with thee. O Lady, teach us to be ever conscious
of the presence of God!

*His is the sea, for He has made it, and the dry land, which
His hands have formed.*

To be the children of wealthy or powerful men, is to be
favored indeed in the eyes of the world. The consciousness of
our privilege of being Your favorite children, O God, our
Creator, will bring far greater happiness. Dear Father, Creator
of land and ocean! We are so proud . . . so happy to be Your

children. We thank You, dear Lord, for the gift of faith which makes us realize Whose children we are. Sad indeed would be our lot, if we felt ourselves to be stages in some evolutionary process . . . complex instruments . . . products of a mechanistic universe . . . bundles of energy projected by chance into space . . . or worse still, if we were sceptical about our own existence as well as its cause. We appreciate all that science has discovered about all the elements. We appreciate more: as Your children, O master Scientist, we seek to know You directly, the ultimate Cause and Creator of all elements. We ponder on the mystery of Your divine Immanence.

Come, let us bow down in worship; let us kneel before the Lord Who made us. For He is our God . . .

Come, let us bow down in worship before Him. With such feelings of love, gratitude, and intense admiration, we must adore Your majestic power and love, O Father, Creator of all things! Adoring Your marvellous power witnessed in the mighty ocean waves . . . the vast expanses of forest and plain . . . the tremendous power of tempests unleashed . . . we fall down reverently before You. Let us kneel before You, the Lord Who made us, for You are our God. We become very timid . . . very small . . . very humble . . . before all the power and beauty reflected in nature. But we marvel still more, O Lord, at Your creation of human nature: we marvel at the mystery of its origin and operation . . . its structure and composition . . . its activity and energy . . . its psychological subtlety . . . its sublime destiny. We beg You, since You have made us for Yourself, O Lord, to keep us ever conscious of Your holy purpose.

and we are the people He shepherds, the flock He guides.

We wish to be numbered as Your people, O Lord . . . Your children . . . as sheep of Your pasture, O divine Good Shepherd. As members of Your flock, let us follow You humbly, submissively, surely, innocently . . . even unto total sacrifice, O divine Shepherd, Who gave Your life for Your sheep!

Hail, Mary, full of grace, the Lord is with thee. O immaculate Mother, help us to follow the Lamb without spot, wherever He goes!

Oh, that today you would hear His voice: "Harden not your hearts as at Meriba, as in the day of Massa in the desert, where your fathers tempted me; they tested Me though they had seen My works."

If grace is given to us, let us not refuse it: if, O Lord, You call us to know You more intimately, to love You more profoundly, to suffer for You, let us accept gladly the trials which You send for our correction and perfection. It is human to murmur, as the Israelites did in the days when You were fitting them for Your work... but true praise of You consists in acting according to supernatural principles rather than from natural motives.

Objectively considered, O Lord, the Israelites who murmured seem a stupid lot. Why did they grumble about trials intended for their own good, especially when they had visible demonstrations of Your almighty power? Nevertheless, we have many more striking indications of Your divine power and goodness. We have manifold examples of Your personal interest in each of us. Do we ever murmur against the manifest arrangements of Your divine providence? or are we intelligent enough to recognize the hand of our Father in all of our daily affairs? Oh, that today we may hear Your voice!

The Lord is with thee. Our Lady, teach us to listen attentively for the voice of God and to unite our wills to His adorable will!

"Forty years I loathed that generation, and I said: 'They are a people of erring heart...

Let us not merit Your rebuke, O God, spoken to these ancients: "Forty years I loathed that generation, and said, 'They are a people of erring heart.'" Are we people of erring hearts? Do we murmur interiorly? or do we feel so smug and self-complacent that we do not admit You into the inner recesses of our being... to the citadel where self is enthroned? Do we forget that You are omniscient... that You see all our false idols and that You discern the inmost secrets of our hearts?

" 'and they know not My ways.'

Lord, we *have* known Your ways, but we have too often, sometimes, alas, deliberately, strolled from Your paths. Rescue us, O divine Saviour, before we incur Your bitter condemnation.

"Therefore I swore in My anger: 'They shall not enter into My rest.' "

In the day of judgment, O Lord, deliver us! From Your wrath, O Lord, deliver us! As we ask You to spare us, to pardon us, to bring us to true penance . . . we beseech You to hear us (Cf. Litany of the Saints).

Hail, Mary, full of grace, the Lord is with thee!

Dear Lady, protect us, that we, too, may always have the Lord with us. Ask for us, O Mother, the grace to cooperate fully with grace . . . that we may be reliable and loyal religious in God's service . . . that we may never incur His everlasting wrath. O Mary, Refuge of sinners, pray for us!

Glory be to the Father, and to the Son, and to the Holy Ghost.

May we know the Persons of the most holy Trinity directly, through Their indwelling in our souls. May we praise Them by our fidelity to grace and our generosity and self-sacrifice.

As it was in the beginning, is now, and ever shall be, world without end.

Thus, may our knowledge and love and praise offered in time be amplified for all eternity. Amen.

The Lord is with thee. Hail, Mary, full of grace, the Lord is with thee.

Our Lady, privileged to be so close to Christ, keep us close to Him! Our Lady, full of grace, help us to profit by every opportunity to grow in grace.

HYMN

*A*DMIRATION, awe, timidity, confusion, and fear could be empty sentiment ... mere emotional effervescence ... and not adoration at all. We contemplate perfect adoration in You, O divine Master and Model of prayer:

The God Whom earth, and sea, and sky
Adore, and laud, and magnify.
Who o'er their threefold fabric reigns,
The Virgin's spotless womb contains.

Omnipotence ...
Deprived of power

The God, Whose will by moon and sun
And all things in due course is done,
Is borne upon a Maiden's breast,
By fullest heavenly grace possessed.

Eternity ...
Produced in time

How blest that Mother, in whose shrine
The great Artificer divine.
Whose hand contains the earth and sky,
Vouchsafed, as in His ark, to lie.

Infinity ...
Confined to space

Blest, in the message Gabriel brought;
Blest, by the work the Spirit wrought;
From whom the great Desire of earth
Took human flesh and human birth.

Divinity ...
Born a Babe

All honor, laud, and glory be,
O Jesu, Virgin born to Thee;
All glory, as is ever meet,
To Father and to Paraclete.[1]

That we might know
And praise
The Victim ... Source ...
And Spirit of Love.

According to our capacity, may we thus love and praise You, Lord ... imitating the wisdom of a Maiden's *fiat* ... docility to the Holy Spirit ... the total renunciation of Jesus Christ, our Master and Model ... as we comprehend more and more clearly Your great gifts bestowed on us, O Father, and the whole Christian paradox proclaimed by the Cross!

---

1 Cf. Dom Matthew Britt, O.S.B., *Hymns of the Breviary and Missal* (New York: Benziger, 1948), pp. 349 and 350.

First Nocturn

Antiphon: *Blessed art thou.*

O Mary, blessed among women, confidently we pray that, through your intercession, our stammering efforts at prayer may be transposed into harmonious canticles of praise.

Psalm 8

O Lord, our Lord, how glorious is Thy name over all the earth!

All created things, O Lord, are a revelation of Your splendor, Your wisdom, Your beauty. Wherever we gaze on the earth, over the sea, aloft in the sky, we must admire the magnitude and the multitude of Your works ... the macrocosmic and the microcosmic perfection of detail. You Who are the Source and Controller of all physical, intellectual, and spiritual energies, must indeed be admired by all intelligent creation. Yes, Lord, You are Lord and Master of the universe, but You are our Lord and Father as well. When we contemplate the wonders of nature and the achievements of science, we are extremely proud of You, our Father, for You have created all things for our welfare!

Thou hast exalted Thy majesty above the heavens.

Engineers who transform the physical environment ... geniuses who effect transformations in the world of ideas ... leaders who transform human society ... all perform magnificent achievements. But Your majesty, O Lord, is exalted above the heavens: it transcends the universe of quantity ... it transcends every conceivable quality. While the architecture of the universe and the beauty of truth are magnificent demonstrations of Your creative power, Your refulgent splendor is most strikingly revealed within the realm of grace. Contemplating Your magnificence, O Lord, may my soul never be content to be absorbed in mere sensible or intelligible phenomena ... but let it be transformed by Your grace.... May all devout souls be transformed by Your grace. May sinners and infidels no longer resist Your grace. May the dying profit by every possible grace. May all members of the Mystical Body receive an abundant increase of Your grace!

Out of the mouths of babes and sucklings Thou hast fashioned praise because of Thy foes, to silence the hostile and the vengeful.

Physical and intellectual maturity are not necessary for development in the life of grace. In fact, divine predilection does
not depend on physical prowess or intellectual acuity. That
faith is far beyond the plane and power of intelligence is most
effectively demonstrated in children who innocently outwit the
keenest created intelligence. Witness the Holy Innocents ...
the heroic virtue of children who are martyrs ... a modern
Saint Maria Goretti. Witness the innocence and the wisdom of
children in prayer and First Communion classes. Teach us,
Lord, to become as little children, that we may enter the kingdom of heaven!

You have fashioned praise ... through the innocence of
Herod's victims ... the courage of the boy Stanislaus ... the
purity of Maria Goretti ... the obedience of Bernadette ... the
faithful prayer of the children of Fatima ... and through the
infinite praise of Gesu Bambino, Divinity incarnate!

"Because of Your foes." Who are these foes? They are the
foes of truth, such as hypocrites, deceivers, perjurers ... foes of
goodness, such as the wicked, boasting of their crimes and con-
temptuous of Your high court ... calculating minds, ignoring
the supernatural light of faith.

"To silence the hostile and the vengeful...." That means,
You have used innocent children to silence the diabolical designs of Lucifer, seducing men by means of their intelligence,
because his own fall was occasioned by pride of intellect. Lord,
silence and destroy in me the subtle demons of conceit, vanity,
pride, ambition ... that Your precious gift of faith may result
in childlike innocence of life, inspired by the wisdom of the
Holy Spirit.

*When I behold Thy heavens, the work of Thy fingers, the
moon and the stars which Thou hast set in place.*

Endowed with the gift of faith, I not only see the heavens,
but I recognize them as products of Your creation ... formed
by Your fingers ... the moon and stars and all nature which
You have established. I gaze upon these, not merely with the
interest and curiosity of a scientist, but with the profound conviction of a true believer.

*What is man that Thou shouldst be mindful of him, or the
son of man that Thou shouldst care for him?*

Physically and chemically, scientists say, man is worth about
ninety-eight cents. In his sensory and instinctive equipment,
he is frequently far inferior to animals. Intellectually, he soon
reaches his limits, no matter what his level of scholarship. The
weakness of his will is lamented even by the saint. What is
man, Lord, that You should care for him?

Beholding the crucifix, or considering any of the several epi-
sodes of Your Passion . . . reflecting on our infidelities and those
of all mankind, we cry out with the Psalmist, "What is man
that You should care for him?" If initially You destined our
first parents for such a privileged state of existence with You,
Lord, in Your eternal abode of love, why have You persisted
in heaping favors upon all mankind since the Fall? especially
since we have proved such stupid ingrates, traitors to Your
love? or why have You not been content with the abundant bestowal of favors, but You have come down in person "to share
our human nature that we might share Your divine nature"
(Offertory prayer of the Mass)? There is only one explanation
. . . though paradoxically enough that is inexplicable to our
finite minds: that answer is the mystery of divine Love . . . an
appreciation of which may be glimpsed in the contemplation of
Christ's Passion . . . in the Sacrifice of the Cross . . . but it needs
to be pondered for all eternity.

What is man that You should care for him? My duties bring
me downtown in the streetcar or bus, into the maelstrom of
morning traffic. Here, all types of humanity are rushing to
wrest from their environment a little bread and butter . . . a
safe refuge for their shelter . . . clothing to keep them warm.
How many of these care about You, O Lord? Certainly, You
care for them, individually and collectively, for You have
planned their existence in Your eternal mind. Nor can I be un-
mindful of them, or indifferently regard them as strangers. I
hasten to pray for each and all of Your children in this car . . .
and for all those we pass along the way: gay-hearted youngsters
en route to school, glamorous and fragile maidens, pale and sad-
faced anonymities, clean-cut, delicate-featured young men,
hard-working laborers already at their toil. Let these be influenced mightily by Your blessings today, Lord. Make them
happy with the happiness of the spirit. The sky-line reveals

a church spire, tipped with a Cross. Yes, O Lord, my request has long ago been anticipated ... You have given more than Your blessing ... You have Yourself come to visit mankind. May we all be mindful of You this day and profit by Your visit!

In the railway station, I again pray for the bedraggled bits of humanity ... the derelicts ... the drunkards ... even the drug addicts ... the forlorn and dejected. I pray also for those eager with excitement of adventure ... those bidding farewell to relatives and friends ... and those starting off on their honeymoon! Let them all be touched today by Your grace. At least, keep them all from committing even one serious sin. Let each one be mindful of You. Let each open the door of his heart for Your visit!

Thou hast made him little less than the angels, and crowned him with glory and honor.

What is man? A being superior to all the rest of Your material creation ... a corporeal and spiritual entity ... only a little less than a pure spirit. Moreover, a creature made to Your own image and likeness! Inanimate and animate substances supply his body with food ... his physical and social environment furnish his mind with truth. His dignity is great in the realm of creation. His position of honor and glory has come directly from Your command to populate the earth and rule over it (Gen. 1: 28).

Thou hast given him rule over the works of Thy hands ...

You have appointed him over the works of Your hands ... that he may scrutinize, analyze, admire them ... that he may select, distribute, develop, and enjoy them ... that he may learn from created things ... to know ... and love ... and serve ... their Creator. Make us conscious, O Father and Creator, of the dignity and honor we have in the universe. Let us exercise over our lower nature the self-control not possible to animals. Let us discipline our minds to recognize the proper hierarchy of values, so that, utilizing material things, we may focus our attention steadily on our spiritual destiny.

putting all things under his feet: All sheep and oxen, yes, and the beasts of the field . . .

You have subjected all things under his feet . . . the dust, common to his clay . . . animals, sharing his sentient life. But You have breathed in man a higher life and made him steward of Your created works . . . Your fields and vineyards . . . Your sheep, oxen, and cattle. He fails in his stewardship . . . blunders in his economy . . . only when he forgets he is Your steward . . . and regards himself as an independent farmer, laborer, mechanic, scientist, soldier, architect, artist, engineer, educator, physician, statesman, or ruler.

The birds of the air, the fishes of the sea, and whatever swims the paths of the seas.

Fish, flesh, and fowl are all ordained for my personal benefit. The joys of hunting and fishing must certainly raise my thoughts to You, O God. Even the morning song of little birds, or their graceful soaring, their unerring instinct of perching on the topmost branch of a tree . . . make one marvel at the care of Your divine providence for all of Your creation . . . "Not a sparrow falls to earth without the Father's knowledge, and the very hairs of your head are numbered" (Matt. 10: 29, 30). The fishing experience of the Apostles taught them many a lesson of Your divine providence. It taught them the lesson of trust . . . prepared them for their high calling as fishers of men.

O Lord, our Lord, how glorious is Thy name in the whole earth!

How glorious are all Your works, signed with the seal of Your divine Authorship! O infinite Majesty! Let our praise of You be not delayed until we experience directly the joy of the Beatific Vision! Your wisdom . . . Your beauty . . . Your goodness . . . Your constant concern for us . . . are all reflected in Your created works. Let us gaze upon these thoughtfully . . . handle them reverently . . . directing them to Your greater glory . . . as wise stewards, destined to adore You for all eternity.

Glory be to the Father, and to the Son, and to the Holy Ghost! As it was in the beginning, is now, and ever shall be, world without end. Amen.

May every atom and substance created by the Father . . . may every soul redeemed by the Son . . . may every thought and desire sanctified by the Holy Ghost . . . represent a million . . . billion . . . trillion *Glorias* that we would wish to utter in praise of the most holy Trinity today!

ANTIPHON: *Blessed art thou among women, and blessed is the fruit of thy womb.*

O Mary, if the divine Majesty has so wonderfully endowed our human nature by making it "a little less than the angels," He has still more abundantly blessed us by making you, the Queen of Angels, the Mother of His Son, and our Blessed Mother as well.

ANTIPHON: *Even as choice myrrh.*

O Mary, breathe upon our humble prayers the fragrance of your virtue, that our words may ascend to heaven as a worthy offering of praise.

PSALM 18

THE heavens declare the glory of God, and the firmament proclaims His handiwork.

Convincing proof of Your existence, O almighty Father, is demonstrated in the majestic sweep of the heavens ... their breath-taking beauty ... infinite variety ... their formidable, ominous power. How can atheists be blind to such evidence of You? Viewing this vast panorama of artistry, Lord, we are especially grateful for the favor You bestow on us. By a divine stratagem, You have seemed to desire to attract our personal attention to You, the Creator of such art. To us, these physical phenomena convey particular messages of Your love. It seems as if You have created them just for us individually and, as a lover who seeks to delight his beloved, You have sought to raise our hearts to You to make us happy. The light of Your truth and the radiance of Your beauty offer not merely proof of Your almighty power, but delectation in Your very Being. The mammoth, star-patterned mystery of the night invites reflection ... provokes speculation ... investigation. If business activities of the day prevent our contemplation of Your divine art and ingenuity, the peace and tranquility of nocturnal heavens equally demonstrate Your glory ... likewise send us Your intimate messages of love ... while You wait for us to look up and admire Your handiwork!

Day pours out the word to day, and night to night imparts knowledge.

Day and night, with alternating chant of praise, proclaim the existence of an intelligent Cause ... nor is their DIVINE OFFICE interrupted for sustenance ... or sleep ... or other necessities proper to human worshippers.

Not a word nor a discourse whose voice is not heard.

This visible and striking demonstration of Your truth, O Lord, is given in silence ... and hence, cannot be misunderstood because of linguistic limitations ... misinterpreted through semantic variations ... or deliberate double-tongued talk ... or obscured by lectures too few, too remote, or too abstract for humble listeners. The intellectual pride and diabolical designs of modern men deliberately use words for a perverse purpose. But Your truth, O Lord, is spoken silently to the mind ... reaches into the recesses of conscience ... is written indelibly in the heart ... is comprehended certainly by the man of faith ... without noise of words.

Through all the earth their voice resounds, and to the ends of the world their message.

Paradoxically enough, these silent utterances of Your truth have been broadcasted to every inhabitant of the earth ... without the media of printing ... or radio ... or television ... oral indoctrination ... or propaganda ... but simply by the quiet manifestation of the order and regularity ... the economy and power ... the wonder and beauty ... the providence and prodigality of nature. All these effects must prompt an intelligent being to seek and worship You, their intelligent, supernatural Cause.

He has pitched a tent there for the sun, which comes forth like the groom from his bridal chamber ...

The natural source of brilliance, light, heat, energy, and power is, of course, the sun. Thus, Lord, You have pitched a tent for the sun. You have hidden from us weak, human creatures ... blinded even by the gleaming radiance of solar energy ... the direct supernatural effulgence of the sun's divine Source. Contemplation of Your effulgent splendor is reserved only for the Beatific Vision, and then according to the measure of one's capacity ... although constant rays of Your divine splendor bring light and strength to countless souls. The sun, invisible in the tent of night, appears in all its gleaming vigor and freshness, diffusing from its heavenly source light and warmth and gladness with each new dawn. In a certain manner, we might reason that the sun, in turn, forms a tabernacle or tent for You, the Lord and Creator, infinitely superior in essence and power to all the works of Your creation. Without faith, man sees only the effects of the sun and walks in spiritual darkness; with faith, man sees beyond the sun, for his soul is illumined with the splendor of Your truth. Presented with truth, yet perversely oblivious of the uncreated Cause, the majority of men tend to worship only the material effects of creation: primitive peoples worshipped the sun, fire, or other forces of nature . . . and modern pseudo-intellectuals prostrate themselves before the sacred shrines of science.

O Lord, You have not been content to remain remotely aloof and hidden from mankind, while demonstrating tremendous physical marvels of Your creative power. Above and beyond physical wonders . . . the sun's rays travelling millions of miles to illuminate and warm the earth . . . are the supernatural wonders of Your love emanating from You, their divine Source, and penetrating the minds and hearts of men. You were not content with an objective illustration of Your existence. There had to be a personal contact made between Creator and creature . . . so that even as the sun here described, You are the Groom Who seeks the love of each human soul. Moreover, not content with loving Your creatures . . . and being loved by them . . . You planned to send Your divine Son to earth to prove Your love for us.

and, like a giant, joyfully runs its course.

Just as the sun with each new day excites human wonder and admiration, as it brings happiness and hope and energy to a lethargic, dreary world, so, O Love incarnate, You have rejoiced in proving Your love for us. You have come as an infant to assume human flesh . . . but Your love was more than human. It reached enormous proportions, as You ran this way of love for us . . . the Way of the Cross . . . the way of total immolation. Contemplating Calvary in the daily Sacrifice of the Mass, we realize that Your love has tremendous power . . . but it is, nevertheless, the gentle, sympathetic, and superhuman love of a divine Personality. Here, indeed, O divine Love, You come forth radiantly from the highest heaven . . . to earth . . . to us . . . to redeem and save us. Moreover, You come to us with each new day in the Holy Sacrifice of the Mass.

At one end of the heavens it comes forth, and its course is to their other end; nothing escapes its heat.

O almighty Father, Your Word made flesh . . . Love incarnate . . . did not simply "share our manhood," but desired us "to share Thy Godhead" (Offertory prayer of the Mass). He has come forth from the highest heaven, but His course is even to the top thereof; that is, He ascends back to heaven, but not without giving us the means to ascend with Him. He has provided us with His Eucharistic sustenance and the other Sacraments, that we might be closely united to You in the contemplation of Your truth . . . in the embrace of Your love. O Jesus, the Way, the Truth, and the Life, help us to run the way to heaven with You. Grant that we may be always faithful to Your love and Your grace, so that those who know You not may learn to know and love You. Inflame our hearts with the fervor of divine love, O Lord, for there is none that can hide from its heat . . . though many resist its beneficial influence.

The law of the Lord is perfect, refreshing the soul; the decree of the Lord is trustworthy, giving wisdom to the simple.

One beneficial influence communicated by You, O Lord, is to be observed in Your law, the law of charity. Promulgated through Your commandments, stressing love of God and love of neighbor, it is perfect and without spot. Since it is established on Your truth and justice, it refreshes souls seeking divine light and affection. Your absolute truth is the basis on which authority for our faith is founded; hence, the child possessing faith in You surpasses the learned of this world in wisdom . . . and the lowly, even illiterate laborer, endowed with belief, holds a spiritual treasure which financial wizards cannot monopolize.

The precepts of the Lord are right, rejoicing the heart; the command of the Lord is clear, enlightening the eye.

The remarkable fact about Your justice, Lord, is that, while it is based on truth, it does not exclude charity or mercy. Innumerable acts of Your justice give to undeserving creatures the right to receive Your benefits, material and spiritual, and make hearts joyful throughout the earth. Your clear commands are filled with love and light and peace, and make us more and more aware of Your justice and truth.

The fear of the Lord is pure, enduring forever; the ordinances of the Lord are true, all of them just.

Love of You is not always sufficient motivation, O Lord, to spur weak human beings to worthy conduct. Reverential fear of You is necessary always, so that we may be impelled towards

the good by our anxiety to avoid evil. Hell furnishes the proper
sanction for Your law, based on eternal truth, and for Your
judgments, based on eternal justice. Grant us the gift of holy
fear, O Lord, to keep us pure forever. From eternal damnation,
O Lord, deliver us! As we ask You to deliver our souls and the
souls of our brethren, relations, and benefactors from eternal
damnation, O Lord, we beseech You to hear us (Cf. Litany of
the Saints)!

*They are more precious than gold, than a heap of purest
gold; sweeter also than syrup or honey from the comb.*

Your spiritual gifts and graces are more to be esteemed than
the most valuable and beautiful of material treasures, and more
delectable than morsels most pleasing to the palate. Faithful
Christians frequently experience the truth of the words uttered
by our Lord. "Take up my yoke upon you, for my yoke is sweet
and my burden light" (Matt. 11: 30).

*Though Thy servant is careful of them, very diligent in keep-
ing them.*

One who truly loves You, O Lord, is very careful to observe
the law of Your love. Even if at times he may have difficulties,
he struggles to obey for the sake of the reward . . . a reward
which "Eye hath not seen, nor ear heard, neither hath it entered
into the heart of any man to conceive" (1 Cor. 2: 9) . . . the reward which is union with You, O God of mercy and of peace!

*Yet who can detect failings? Cleanse me from my unknown
faults!*

How can I so thoughtlessly violate the law of love? How can
I so easily forget the many favors heaped on me? Why is not
the fear of Your just judgments effective in making me recoil
from such ingratitude? Why do I succumb so readily to the
snares of sin? From the insidious, secret sins, deliver me, O
Lord! First, help me recognize the slow, steady surrender that
my soul makes to Satan by satisfying the senses. From subtle
suggestions of pride . . . from base ambition and covetousness
. . . from self-centered sins of the mind and obstinate perversity
of will . . . cleanse me, O Lord! If it is so difficult to realize the
external faults which make me disagreeable to others, how hard
it is to know my interior defects displeasing to You, Lord. With
St. Augustine, I cry, "O Lord, let me know myself that I may
know Thee!"

From wanton sin especially, restrain Thy servant; let it not rule over me.

From the lack of restraint which gives bad example to others, preserve me, O Lord! Make me ever aware of my responsibility in regard to my neighbor. If by my levity I have led him astray, or scandalized him by my foolish conduct, or prevented his praiseworthy acts by ironic remarks or little encouragement . . . if I have scoffed at those who tried to practice virtue, or criticized those upholding high principles . . . for these I pray, as well as for those whom more prayers might rescue this day from evil. I pray for the sick, suffering physical or mental distress . . . for those victims of misplaced zeal, in or out of concentration camps . . . that they may bear their pain heroically . . . for those concerned about the fate of their families, friends and relatives . . . for the holy souls, suffering in purgatory . . . for sinners on earth, that they may be converted to Your ways . . . for the virtuous, that they may become more closely united to You and glorify You . . . for souls whom prayer or good example might lead to dedicate their lives in a special way to You.

Then shall I be blameless and innocent of serious sin.

If I am not ruled by these hydra-headed monsters of sins . . . the hidden sins which sabotage moral integrity and the sins which scandalize other souls . . . then shall I live a pure life, pleasing to You, O Lord. By Your grace then, deliver me from the greatest evil . . . the capital sin of pride, leading to deceit, ingratitude, violence, despair, deicide.

Let the words of my mouth and the thought of my heart find favor before Thee, O Lord, my Rock and my Redeemer.

Let the Sacrament of Penance cleanse me from sin and purify my soul for Your advent, O Lord, "that the words of my mouth and the thought of my heart find favor before Thee." Purity increases the power of praise and prepares the way for meditation . . . contemplation . . . and continued union with You.

"O Lord, my Rock and my Redeemer," help me to be vigilant, to resist the enticements of sin . . . to practice penance . . . to keep my soul pure and pleasing to You . . . to capitalize spiritually on the fruits of Your redemption . . . to share in Your redemptive offering . . . that others may gain more light to know and love You, and glorify Your name throughout eternity!

Glory be to the Father, and to the Son, and to the Holy Ghost.

And may this glory be increased by geometric progression, a hundred million, billion times. But an increase in quantity is not sufficient. May it increase in quality. May it be multiplied by all the choirs of angels and all the saints enjoying supernal bliss ... by all who live primarily to praise You, O most holy Trinity! *As it was in the beginning, is now, and ever shall be, world without end.* May this praise be continued ... intensified and magnified ... for all eternity. *Amen.*

ANTIPHON: *Even as choice myrrh, thou gavest the odor of sweetness, O holy Mother of God.*

O Mary immaculate, preserved from the slightest taint of sin, pray that we may be preserved from serious sin and may grow in virtues pleasing to your divine Son.

ANTIPHON: *Before the couch.*

Kneeling before you, O blessed Mother, we ask you to teach us the melody of heavenly music that we may forever sing joyful hymns in praise of the Lord.

PSALM 23

*T*HE *Lord's are the earth and its fullness; the world and those who dwell in it.*

Who can dispute Your Creator's claim, O God? Your priority of property title to the earth? its produce? its people? their hearts? their minds? their souls? As a triumphant Conqueror, O Lord, You rule the universe and all its inhabitants.

Strange fantasy of empire builders, who seek to usurp Your place, O God, as master of the world ... to dominate human lives, as if they existed merely to serve tyrannical power! Unsound system of politics, which places over others those who obtain power through base chicanery! Queer economy, which allows earth's produce to spoil, while thousands of Your creatures starve! Superficial science, which probes the secrets of earth and ignores You, their divine Author! Inadequate education, which teaches everything but the only thing that matters! Blind philosophy, which dares to explain so many truths, yet does not recognize You, O supreme Wisdom! Human blunderers have succeeded in causing much chaos in this world, but, O Lord, You will triumph over conquerors and rulers ... over economists and scientists ... over educators and philosophers

and all Your creatures endowed with free will. You are triumphant now, for nothing occurs without Your permissive will.

The man of faith reveres You, Lord, and respects Your gifts.
He is conscious that his fellow-men are made to Your image
and likeness. He labors to acquire the necessities of life for
himself and his family. He prays earnestly for his daily bread
and relies trustingly on Your divine providence. Out of his
abundance he gives generously to the poor and needy. He does
not try to wrest Your power from You ... or Your property ...
or Your right to our worship. He knows that the earth is Yours
and the fullness thereof.

*For He founded it upon the seas and established it upon the
rivers.*

Although the simple man of faith may lack the intellectual
polish of pedants, or the impressive skill of technicians, he
knows the story of Genesis. He believes the account of Creation.
He is not like the modern savant, sneering and skeptical about
everything supernatural ... nor is he so immersed in matter
that he denies the needs of the spirit.

*Who can ascend the mountain of the Lord? or who may
stand in His holy place?*

The weary farmer pushing his plow? the laborer, mechanic,
or tradesman, railroad worker, miner, bus driver, toiling away
yet always so dependable, loyal and cheerful? the stenographer
or clerk, ever faithful to duty? professional men and women,
merchants, executives, civic leaders, performing numerous hidden acts of charity and bearing heavy responsibilities? Who
can ascend Your mountain, O Lord?

*He whose hands are sinless, whose heart is clean, who desires
not what is vain, nor swears deceitfully to his neighbor.*

The Psalmist answers his own query. Undoubtedly, all these
people just mentioned have the natural virtues which are the
foundation for progress in holiness. Moreover, we all have the
opportunity to "ascend the mountain of the Lord," that is, to
enter into Your tabernacled Presence, O Lord, and even to receive You as the Guest of our hearts ... provided that we are
innocent in our thoughts and actions and do not desire "what
is vain," that is, provided that we act according to the proper
hierarchy of values established by faith. As we fulfill con-
scientiously our duties to You, O God, we must also recognize
and observe the principles of justice in our relations with our
fellow-men.

The man pure in body and mind will appear in Your sacred Presence, O divine Truth... for he never loses sight of the noble purpose which motivates his life and he is, therefore, less attracted to things of earth. The man poor in spirit, who remains ever conscious of his sublime spiritual destiny... who practices obedient submission to the will of Your providence ... who is loyal and generous to his brothers on earth as well as to You, his Father in heaven... he will be the person privileged to look upon You, O Lord.

He shall receive a blessing from the Lord, a reward from God his Saviour.

He will be richly rewarded in spirit, according to his renunciation of vain material attractions. He who resists valiantly the comforts of life here will enjoy abundant spiritual luxuries. He who observes the laws of justice and fraternal charity will receive Your blessing, O eternal Father.

Such is the race that seeks for Him, that seeks the face of the God of Jacob.

Yes, even those who are seeking false values today are really seeking You, O God, but they stop before they reach You. They are so dazzled by Your gifts that they lack the light to discern You, O divine Giver. They are seeking happiness, but do not know where to find it. Men endowed with the gift of faith know where and how to find genuine happiness... in You alone. Religious men and women and souls especially chosen by You, O Lord, are given particular advantages and graces that help them to discern spiritual values. Will it not be tragic, if the zeal of Your favored members of the Mystical Body of Christ does not excel the ardor and energy of those motivated by unworthy purposes?... if the person vowed to poverty, chastity, and obedience, pursues futile objects... acquires a multitude of personal possessions... allows his mind to be adulterated by vain or useless thoughts... secretly hopes for positions of influence... or comfort... or power... is self-complacent concerning his achievements... or jealous and envious of his neighbor? Will the religious expecting to ascend Your mountain, O Lord, not suffer a tragic disappointment, if his countenance... accustomed to look *comfortably* upon the face of Christ... gazes into Your mirror of truth, only to find reflected there the lineaments of Lucifer?

Lift up, O gates, your lintels; reach up, ye ancient portals, that the King of glory may come in!

Open wide the gates of your hearts, O sons and daughters of divine adoption, royalty of God, heirs of the kingdom of heaven through Baptism, members of the Mystical Body of Christ, chosen souls whom God has favored! Allow this King of glory to come in ... not as a stranger ... or formal guest ... but as an intimate Friend Who comes to conquer the citadel of self-complacency ... to demolish the pride and ambition which would contest His exclusive rights over your souls! And be lifted up, O ancient gates ... rusty with habits of self-indulgence and sin ... to admit this King of glory.

Who is this King of glory? the Lord, strong and mighty, the Lord, mighty in battle.

He is the King of kings ... invincible but patient, as He waits for the complete surrender of our hearts.

Lift up, O gates, your lintels; reach up, ye ancient portals, that the King of glory may come in!

Lift up the gates ... the iron curtains of your hearts, O rulers and leaders of earth ... and the King of glory shall enter in. Open your minds to His truth ... your wills to His grace ... your affections to His love. Conquer the demons of pride and prejudice and perversity of spirit. Pray for light ... and may your prayer be heard on high! Then the King of glory shall enter into the temple of your souls.

Who is this King of glory? The Lord of hosts; He is the King of glory.

Who is the King of glory? The Lord Who created heaven and earth and all things ... the Prince of peace ... Who said "My kingdom is not of this world" ... the divine Ruler Who seeks to conquer you. May His kingdom come on earth as it is in heaven. May His triumph over you be eternally glorious!

Glory be to the Father, and to the Son, and to the Holy Ghost. As it was in the beginning, is now, and ever shall be, world without end. Amen.

May all men on earth come to adore You and love You and praise You, even as the angels and saints, who spend their whole eternity glorifying You in the profound mystery of the most holy Trinity. *Amen.*

ANTIPHON: *Before the couch of this Virgin sing to us often songs sweet and solemn.*

O Queen of the angelic choirs, amplify and vivify and multiply our feeble utterances that they may be transformed into celestial harmonies agreeable to the divine Majesty!

VERSICLE: *Grace is poured forth on thy lips.* RESPONSE: *Therefore God has blessed thee forever.*

By your words and by your actions, O Mary, you have always shown full correspondence with the grace bestowed on you. Pray that we may imitate your example according to our capacity and likewise secure the favor of the Lord!

Our Father (silently).

Our Father, Who art in heaven . . . grant us the grace, not only to observe the universal law of charity, but keep us keenly conscious of our particular dignity as members of the Mystical Body of Christ, Who first taught us this prayer, and by Whose merits we have become privileged to become Your children.

And lead us not into temptation. But deliver us from evil.

Especially lead us not into the temptation of forgetting that we are Your children and that our fellow men are also Your children . . . all dependent on Your paternal care. Deliver us, O Father, from the hollow bitterness and despair confronting those who seek mere physical rejuvenation in their advancing years.

ABSOLUTION

By the prayers and merits of the Blessed Mary ever Virgin and of all the Saints, may the Lord bring us to the kingdom of Heaven. Amen.

O Mary, Mediatrix of all graces, we pray your intercession for all those souls who have not the faith in the one, true God . . . or for those souls who have, through some sad perversity of will, abandoned it. We pray for these and for all who labor in mission fields at home and abroad . . . and also for all the faithful, that they may welcome the Christ Child as King of their hearts.

Pray, Lord, a blessing . . . the blessing of pondering well the mystery we are about to hear.

May the Virgin Mary with her loving Child bless us. Amen.
May we profit by the lessons taught us by Wisdom incarnate!

ADVENT LESSONS

LESSON I: (Luke 1: 26-28)

𝒯 HE *Angel Gabriel was sent from God into a city of Galilee
called Nazareth, to a Virgin espoused to a man whose name was
Joseph, of the house of David, and the Virgin's name was Mary.
And the Angel being come in said to her: Hail, full of grace,
the Lord is with thee, blessed art thou among women.*

A skeptical generation smiles at this simple credence in
spirits, O God! How can a generation which has witnessed
gigantic strides in science ... the recording and broadcasting of
the human voice, the televising of human activity, the wondrous
effects of electric and atomic power ... doubt the possibility of
supernatural beings? The believer knows from revelation that
angels minister before Your throne, O divine Majesty! They
fulfill the office of guardian for each soul created in this world,
and communicate divine messages to man, as their very name
angel suggests. However, sophomoric Christians are quite oblivious of the official function of angels. They are likely to
slight these powerful advocates in heaven, because they prefer
to pray to someone with greater spiritual "influence." Our
Blessed Mother was better informed in matters of faith. Not
only did she recognize the Angel as Your ambassador, dear
Lord, but she received him with all respect and humility.

In contrast to the worldly standards set up by modern critics,
the angel makes no comment on Mary's physical attractiveness
... her features, figure, hairdo, attire, carriage ... but stresses
the essential value of her character, indicating her consequent
nearness to You, her God, and her superiority to all other
women. As I stand before my Guardian Angel ... do the gifts
of grace used to spiritual advantage in my soul impress him
... or is he disgusted by my fussiness over superficialities? Oh,
Angel Guardian, all the choirs of Angels, and Mary, Queen of
Angels, kindly pray that I may keep ever in mind the one
essential value of life ... growth in God's grace and union with
Him.

Significant in this account of the Angel Gabriel's visit to
Mary, O loving Father, is the sobriety and precision of detail
which marks an event arranged by Your providence thousands
of years previous to its actuality: Your divine Son was to be
of the royal line of David. This is more apparent in the
following:

LESSON II: (Luke 1: 29-33)

And when she heard these things, she was troubled at his saying, and thought with herself what manner of salutation this should be. And the Angel said to her: Fear not, Mary, for thou hast found grace with God. Behold, thou shalt conceive in thy womb, and shalt bring forth a Son, and thou shalt call His name Jesus. He shall be great, and shall be called the Son of the Most High. And the Lord God shall give unto Him the throne of David His father; and He shall reign in the house of Jacob forever, and of His Kingdom there shall be no end.

Reflection on the circumstances of one's own birth, education, vocation, and special advantages or disadvantages will demonstrate to a person endowed with faith that Your divine providence, O heavenly Father, is concerned with each created soul and has planned even apparently trivial details of its life and its work from all eternity. Pondering on this tremendous fact, of Your particular interest in each of us, one might well be troubled, as Mary was, when she heard the salutation from on high. But the Angel said: "Fear not, Mary, for thou hast found grace with God." Thus, again the Angel stresses the important fact of making good use of the grace You bestow on the soul. Mary, immaculate Virgin full of grace, was to become Mother of Your divine Son. We know not what special work You have in mind for us, O divine Master, but we know You desire us to be fruitful in Christian virtue.

LESSON III: (Luke 1: 34-38)

And Mary said to the Angel: How shall this be done, because I know not man? And the Angel answering, said to her: The Holy Ghost shall come upon thee, and the power of the Most High shall overshadow thee; and therefore also the Holy which shall be born of thee shall be called the Son of God. And behold, thy cousin Elizabeth, she also hath conceived a son in her old age; and this is the sixth month with her that is called barren; because no word shall be impossible with God. And Mary said: Behold the handmaid of the Lord; be it done to me according to Thy word.

Not expecting such a signal honor, Mary had long ago made plans for the cultivation of her own spiritual life. Obviously, a primary factor in her sanctification was renunciation, since, as she indicated to the Angel, she had a vow of virginity and had no intention of violating it. When the Angel explained the Holy Ghost's operation which was to effect this wondrous event, and when he cited other evidence of Your divine intervention in referring to her cousin Elizabeth, Mary humbly complied with Your will, O Lord, and hastened to assist Elizabeth. These lessons of renunciation and ready resignation to Your adorable will through love, coupled with a steadfast belief in You and trust in Your divine providence and power, along with personal works of fraternal charity, are virtues the modern world needs to acquire. They are virtues which I must acquire; for without them, there can be no heroic sanctity.

But Thou, O Lord, have mercy on us. Thanks be to God.

Fittingly does each lesson close with a plea for divine mercy; for, meditating on this Gospel story, we become quite conscious of how much we need Your grace and Your indulgence. As the choir responds *Deo gratias,* we become grateful for all Your past gifts of grace, O God, for ourselves and those for whom we pray ... for the grace given to our Blessed Mother ... for her prompt submission to Your will, which gave us our Saviour and Redeemer and all Your precious gifts bestowed through the medium of the Sacraments. We breathe a prayer to our Lady, Mediatrix of all graces, that the grace of God in us be not in vain (Cf. Paul 2 Corinthians 6: 1). We ask her, O Holy Spirit, to help us to cooperate with You in producing the features of Christ in our souls ... so that, more and more identified with Him, we may offer to the eternal Father the complete oblation of our love.

SECOND NOCTURN

ANTIPHON: *In thy beauty.*

In your beauty, O Lady, interior as well as exterior, proceed to make effectual my desires for the cultivation of a sturdy, Christlike life.

Psalm 44

*M*ʏ *heart overflows with a goodly theme; as I sing my ode
to the King* . . .

Participation in public worship is not the only way I wish
to manifest devotion to You, O my Lord! Those vocal prayers
are mere echoes of the intense love filling my heart. This love
cannot be confined to words alone, but wants to express itself
in every action of the day . . . writing, teaching, sewing, cooking, serving others in any way . . . and all those hidden works
which I dedicate to You, my King!

My tongue is nimble as the pen of a skillful scribe.

As I utter words of praise, I do not stop to ponder the deep
meaning of each; yet I proceed as deliberately and seriously
as one who writes quickly, after previously considering the re-
quirements of the undertaking at hand. Moreover, launching
into the declaration of Your praises, Lord, it is with an *allegro
tempo* I must reflect joy and fervor of spirit; for a *largo* movement is ill-suited to hymns of praise. It seems now that I perceive more and more clearly the meaning of Your words in
Holy Scripture, in quite another fashion than the way in which
they usually are applied: "The letter killeth, but the spirit
quickeneth" (2 Corinthians 3: 6).

*Fairer in beauty art Thou than the sons of men; grace is
poured out upon Thy lips; thus God has blessed Thee forever.*

O incarnate Word, most beautiful among the sons of men,
perfect image of the Source of all goodness and grace, eternally
loved and praised by the Father and the Holy Ghost, inundate
our souls with the abundant treasures of Your grace, that we
may discern and appreciate genuine beauty, ever strive to attain it through the imitation of Your life on earth, and eternally
contemplate its essence in the glory of the Beatific Vision!

*Gird Thy sword upon Thy thigh, O mighty One! In Thy
splendor and Thy majesty, ride on triumphant.*

Conquer all our stubborn resistance and evil tendencies with
the sword of the Spirit, O most mighty One . . . for surrender to
You must be unreserved and complete. Arm us with the armor
of truth and justice. Instill in our lukewarm spirits the valor of
loyal and distinguished Christian soldiers!

Surrender to Your irresistible loveliness is sweet, transform-
ing pain into joy. In Your splendor and Your majesty, ride on
triumphant over all hearts . . . over all nations . . . over all peoples . . . bringing them salvation! Grant me that missionary

zeal which reaches out to every soul on earth, to pray for them and help to save them. Grant me that ardor of love which gazes sadly on the tragic and irreparable loss of all those good but mediocre souls who could love You more, but lackadaisically love You less! By unremitting prayer and sacrifice, may I bring all souls closer to You!

In the cause of truth and for the sake of justice; and may Thy right hand show Thee wondrous deeds.

Bring them the salvation of Your truth and the graces of Your redemption. Extend over them the mildness and justice of Your reign. And Your right hand, always accustomed to perform works of goodness and mercy ... to heal the sick ... give sight to the blind ... to bless all, even Your enemies ... and to execute more remarkable wonders in the realm of the spirit ... this right hand shall triumph by wondrous deeds, which will win the hearts of men.

Thine arrows are sharp; peoples are subject to Thee; the King's enemies lose heart.

The keen arrows of Your truth and goodness and justice shall pierce the clouds of ignorance, suspicion, prejudice, and doubt. Truth will prevail. Hasten the day, O Lord, when all people shall adore You fervently as members of the one, true faith!

Thy throne, O God, stands forever and ever; a tempered rod is Thy royal scepter.

The instability of human government is the record of all history, but the immutability of Your truth, O God, is a guarantee of eternal justice. Scandalous corruption in high places is consequent to a series of lesser corruptions in lower places. It arises from those who view expediency as the criterion of truth, alleged to have but an instrumental value. Yet, O God, the infallibility of Your justice is based on objective truth, which stresses the necessity for moral integrity. Equity under Your rule ensures complete confidence ... it stimulates souls of all economic and social strata to strive for that perfection which alone can lead to peace and happiness in the contemplation of Your Word.

Thou lovest justice and hatest wickedness; therefore God, Thy God, has anointed Thee with the oil of gladness above Thy fellow kings.

Your word, our Lord, makes definite and clear the utter incompatibility of truth and iniquity. Therefore, eternal Truth, the Father, has anointed You, the Word, with the unction of perfect happiness, resulting from the complete satiation of the spiritual faculties in truth and goodness. Since You are the divine image of absolute Truth and Goodness, You are the divine personification of absolute Happiness. If Your poor human brothers had even the slightest acquaintance with You, knowing You as You really are, they could not rest until they would abandon everything in pursuit of You. Truly have You spoken from the Cross, "Father, forgive them, for they know not what they do" (Luke 23: 24).

With myrrh and aloes and cassia Thy robes are fragrant; from ivory palaces string music brings Thee. joy.

But, O Lord, the truth which shines with such splendor is only one of Your divine perfections. Other attributes exude their delicate and poignant fragrance from Your garments, that is, under the various manifestations of Your goodness during Your life on earth. The myrrh, suggesting as it does Your burial, may be looked upon as a symbol of the virtues of Your hidden life. It reminds us, too, of the complete sacrifice, "even unto death," for all who would imitate You perfectly. Aloes, the perfumed wood of an Indian tree[1], may recall that, although Architect of the universe, You have assumed the hard, rough, exacting labors of a carpenter during long hours with persevering efforts to serve a none too gracious public; or, it may remind us of the tree of the Cross, instrument of Your bitter Passion and our glorious Redemption, the tree of Your humility and of our base ingratitude. Cassia, fragrant root of the Kashmir plant[1], used for incense, reminds us of the contemplation and prayer characteristic of Your life on earth . . . the spirit of which we must imitate, if we are to make any progress in Christian holiness. The houses of ivory symbolize the purity of the life shared by all Your children. The string music suggests the exquisite and harmonious joys experienced by those who live close to You.

The daughters of kings come to meet Thee; the queen takes her place at Thy right hand in gold of Ophir.

Holy Mother Church, Your spouse, stands at Your right hand, tenderly devoted to Your will, anxious to extend Your reign, and ready to assume the manifold responsibilities of her high office. Her golden robe is indicative of her royalty. The

---

1 Cf. Very Rev. Charles J. Callan, O.P., *The New Psalter* (New York: Wagner, 1949), p. 142, n. 9.

daughters of kings are her children, heirs of heaven, and they symbolize the abundant variety of holiness observed in her saints.

Hear, O daughter, and see; turn thine ear, forget thy people and thy father's house.

Under the maternal guidance of the Church and her ordained representatives, individual souls are summoned to render special service to You, O Lord. This religious vocation requires an ear attuned to receive Your sacred whisperings, an eye accustomed to discern Your beauty, and a will prepared to renounce even worthy attachments, solely for the love and desire of You. This invitation comes directly from You, Lord, as You speak softly the words: "Hear, O daughter, and see; turn thine ear, and forget thy people and thy father's house, and anything and anybody that will interfere with total surrender to Me."

So shall the King desire thy beauty; for He is thy Lord, and thou must worship Him.

Then, O Creator and King of all beauty, You will be enamored with the beauty of true religious souls, who renounce material wealth through the vow of poverty, legitimate sense satisfactions through the vow of chastity, and freedom of their own wills through the vow of obedience. You love with a special love those souls who are consecrated entirely to You, because You are their Lord and they adore You in spirit and in truth, in theory and in fact.

And the city of Tyre is here with gifts; the rich among the people seek Thy favor.

Not merely religious, but all souls, rich in grace, who have successfully traded their material possessions for spiritual goods, will dedicate themselves to You under the protection of Mary, Your Mother, as their Queen. Through her, O Lord, they will offer You all their thoughts, words, actions, desires, achievements, handicaps, even failures, that these further investments may steadily yield exceedingly profitable spiritual returns. Religious can best fulfill their sublime vocation through unremitting efforts to imitate Mary. Lay apostles, under Mary's guidance, will find their devotion to Your cause exceedingly fruitful.

All glorious is the King's daughter as she enters; her raiment is threaded with spun gold.

The world recommends glamor as the essential ingredient of beauty, O Lord, but the world does not recognize the dignity of the Christian, the royal heir to Your kingdom of heaven, whose conduct must be regulated by the principle of *noblesse oblige.* Your daughter, O King of kings, does not depend on physical attractiveness or seductive snares. Her beauty is of the moral and spiritual order and most of it is imperceptible to the senses. Nevertheless, it is glorious. Her raiment is made of spun gold; that is, she exhibits in her manners and habits the precious quality of her personal handiwork and taste. Hence, O Lord, in spite of the unfortunate external faults we observe in some religious ... blemishes permitted lest they become too proud ... glimpses into their interior life reveal in the realm of sanctifying grace the genuine beauty whereby they please You, their divine Lover. They persevere in offering their greatest treasures to glorify You Whose magnificent splendor is variously reflected in the diverse traits and types of their respective personalities.

In embroidered apparel she is borne in to the King; behind her the virgins of her train are brought to Thee.

Although contemplation of You is the "better part" (Luke 10: 42), Lord, the zealous religious is most desirous to communicate the truth comprehended and to share with others the happiness realized. Therefore, the worthy religious will, through her active works of mercy, influence pure souls to keep close to You. By her example, she will encourage all with whom she comes in contact to serve You, their King, with great fidelity, according to their respective vocations. By prayer and good example, O Lord, may I be a worthy religious in this respect. I pray especially now for all children who are born today, that good religious influences may favor them and lead them along the paths of high sanctity during their lives.

They are borne in with gladness and joy; they enter the palace of the King.

People are very sad frequently when they see aspirants to a religious community leave the world to dedicate themselves entirely to Your service, O God. If they could know the truth, there is no greater joy on earth, no greater peace and happiness, than the privilege of dwelling under the same roof with You, our divine Lord in the Blessed Sacrament. Souls endowed with a religious vocation enter Your temple, O King, in joy and rejoicing ... not because they lack sincere affection for their relatives and friends, but rather because they are enthusiastically in love with You, their Lord.

The place of thy fathers thy sons shall have; thou shalt make them princes through all the land.

To take the places of Your Apostles and early disciples and Fathers of the Church, younger men are ordained for the sacred ministry. These will carry out Your direction, "Go, therefore, and teach ye all nations" (Mark 16: 15). We pray daily that You will send many laborers into Your vineyard. We pray for our Holy Father, for our bishops, missionaries at home and abroad, and for all priests valiantly laboring as other Christs throughout the world.

I will make thy name memorable through all generations; therefore shall nations praise thee forever and ever.

As members of the Mystical Body of Christ, may all the faithful join with the priest at the Offertory of the Mass, placing all their prayers, works, and sufferings on the paten when it is raised at Your sacrificial altar, O God! Through You, O divine High Priest, spotless Victim and pure Oblation, may they offer acts of adoration and praise, resounding to the glory of the ever blessed Trinity!

Glory be to the Father.

Glory be to the Father Who created us, to the Son Who redeemed us, and to the Holy Ghost Who sanctifies us. May our lisping attempts at prayer and praise be recorded and treasured forever in the divine memory, even as the imperfect articulations of children are recalled and appreciated by fond and loving parents!

ANTIPHON: *In thy beauty and comeliness go on, advance prosperously, and reign.*

O Lady, reflecting in a finite but superior way the beauty and attractiveness of infinite truth and justice, go on by your intercession, spreading the light and the love of God through the world . . . advance prosperously with the conversion of sinners . . . and reign as Queen, not only of all saints but of all Christians who aspire to sanctity.

ANTIPHON: *God will help her.*

God will help each soul through you, O Blessed Mother, Mediatrix of all graces, since He is always with you. Intercede for us often, therefore, O Lady of perpetual succour!

PSALM 45

*G*OD *is our refuge and our strength, an ever-present help in distress.*

In times of severe trials and tribulations, faith provides the only real consolation, for it teaches us to rely solely on You, God, our refuge and strength. In You we can have complete trust and confidence, for You will never fail us.

The Hebrews, rescued from severe trials and tribulations, were enabled to appreciate Your benefits, Lord. Subjected to suffering, they learned to rely on You, the one Reality superior to it. Likewise, Your sustaining hand is tangible to heroic Christians who suffer: physical pain is endured in union with Christ's sacred Passion. When bereavement bows their heads in sorrow, grace sings its *Sursum corda.* Trouble and worry and fear make them trust more firmly in Your providence Doubts and spiritual trials increase their faith and cause them to cling more closely to You, Lord. Intellectual cynics may cite this Psalm as evidence of escapism in religion. But who are the real escapists, O Lord? Christian ascetics, worshipping You, their Creator? or these rationalistic, luxury-loving adorers of gadgets, seeking escape from You, the eternal Reality?

You, O God, are a refuge and strength, helping us to solve the major issues of life. In these days of anxiety and strife. You are the only true and abiding Reality, timeless and change less, amidst a confused mass of false and fluctuating values.

Therefore we fear not, though the earth be shaken and mountains plunge into the depths of the sea.

Therefore, O almighty Protector, we shall not fear the threat of disastrous upheavals of the physical order. Rather, we shall pray daily for an increase of faith ... for the faith of such quality as You declared could "remove mountains" (Matt. 17: 19). Thus, let our troublous times be spiritually salutary, O God!

Though its waters rage and foam and the mountains quake at its surging.

The tumultuous waters of life swirling around us, the mountainous problems, discouraging all progress, are all under Your control, O omnipotent Father, our Creator, ever solicitous for the welfare of Your children. If You allow us to know the dangers, the temptations, and the difficulties of this world, it is so that we may learn the value of the virtue of hope. We pray daily for an increase of hope, that we may abandon ourselves confidently and unreservedly to Your solicitous care, O loving Father!

The Lord of hosts is with us; our stronghold is the God of Jacob.

Almighty God, You will protect us: You have kept Your covenant with the ancients. You have promised to remain with the Church all days to the end of the world (Matt. 28: 20).

There is a stream whose runlets gladden the city of God, the holy dwelling of the most High.

In contrast to the noise and tumult and strife of the world, is Your city, O God, refreshed by the gentle stream of divine grace. There, amidst peace and tranquility and order, O most High, Source of all goodness and grace, You have established Your abode. Our Blessed Mother, humble channel of grace to us, knew intimately Your Presence. The soul in the state of sanctifying grace also tabernacles You, Lord. May all souls come to know this interior joy! We pray for an increase of sanctifying grace, that we may imitate our Blessed Lady, and thus become more and more pleasing to You, O Lord!

God is in its midst; it shall not be disturbed; God will help it at the break of dawn.

Your kingdom, O God, cannot be disturbed, because it is defended by Your divine Presence. You will protect it in the morning early, that is, before the insidious attacks of the wicked can do any harm. The privilege of the Immaculate Conception of the Blessed Virgin is a striking example of this. Likewise, Your kingdom within us is defended by You, Lord, since You endow the soul with prevenient grace to help it resist its enemies. We pray for this grace for ourselves and others, that we may be adequately prepared for the spiritual combat that can lead us to sanctity.

Though nations are in turmoil, kingdoms totter, His voice resounds, the earth melts away.

O Lord, we are very weak creatures: in spite of astute human planning, United Nations' organizations, peace parleys, arbitration boards, collective bargaining, nations are troubled by manifold evils. Kingdoms of the earth totter and fall. You rarely perform miracles to protect us from our human blunderings. Nevertheless, You can and will assist us by an influx of grace ... to enable us to struggle valiantly for Your sake and thus win greater glory for You and greater merit for ourselves in heaven.

The Lord of hosts is with us; our stronghold is the God of Jacob.

O Lord almighty, You are with us. Whom then shall we fear? O God of Jacob, You are our Defender. For centuries You have guided Your people in the way of eternal truth. Will You do less for us? To test his courage and strength, You allowed Jacob to wrestle with an angel, Lord, but You watched over him and guided him and all his posterity. In the struggles of life, we know You are watching over us, too, and we know that You will come to our assistance when we most need Your gracious help.

Come! behold the deeds of the Lord, the astounding things He has wrought on earth: He has stopped wars to the end of the earth . . .

Contemplation of the works of nature . . . the sky, the ocean, the sweeping vistas of mountain, valley, and plain, life in all forms and stages . . . reveals Your omnipotence, O Lord! You can make wars to cease even to the end of the earth. Nevertheless, O Prince of peace, You do not desire a forced peace, superimposed from above, but rather a peace that develops and grows within each man's heart, when his conscience is free from sin and he has won Your friendship. According to Your words, O Lord, Your Father could have sent ten legions of angels against Your enemies to prevent Your Passion and Death. In Your inscrutable wisdom, You preferred to suffer for love of us, to give us the merits of Your Crucifixion and the Holy Sacrifice of Calvary. We find it hard to understand war or suffering, of course, but we can appreciate better the value of perfect peace, or love, or wisdom, when we know the sacrifices and struggles involved in attaining them.

More admirable than Your visible wonders in the world, O
God, are the invisible wonders You effect in human hearts.
Your providential arrangement of the pattern of our lives offers
many evidences of Your personal interest in each one of us. We
scarcely realize the blessings of the peace which You bring,
until we gaze into the eyes of those who know You not. Then
we know that the peace You bring to earth means more than
a mere cessation of hostilities . . . a negative peace; rather, it is
the peace which recognizes You as our Father, and all men
as our brothers whom we are willing and eager to assist . . . the
peace that springs from perfect charity. We pray for this gift
of charity. We pray that all men may come to know this peace
. . . the peace which the world cannot give. Then and then only,
we realize, will wars cease even to the end of the earth.

*the bow He breaks; He splinters the spears; He burns the
shields with fire.*

O almighty Father, You will destroy jet, atom, and hydrogen
bombs and all the modern weapons of warfare. You can easily
protect us in every type of combat; from espionage and sub-
versive activities, and from germ warfare, during an armed
truce, undeclared war, psychological warfare, and sanguinary
encounters. However, O Lord, You are not concerned so much
about the missiles that assail the body, as those that may pene-
trate to the soul. The moral weapons that weaken our will,
flatter our vanity, nurture our pride, induce sloth or cowardice,
stimulate our passions, will act like radar on the armor of the
unwary. Our spiritual armor will render us quasi-invulnerable,
however, if we endeavor to execute Your divine commands in
this battle of life.

*Desist! and confess that I am God, exalted among the nations,
exalted upon the earth.*

As valiant and loyal soldiers of Christ, of course, we are eager
to have the superiority of our heavenly Leader of the Church
militant recognized throughout the world. But Lord, You require patience among Your followers. You say, "Desist! and
confess that I am God!" Your meaning is clear. If we behave,
not as barbarians, but as Christians, our example will offer
convincing proof that You are God. Then eventually all peoples will come to acknowledge Your power. You will be exalted
and praised and glorified by all peoples throughout the earth.
No . . . You do not wish our zeal to take the form of anger, calling fire and brimstone on the heads of Your enemies. You do
not wish us to take up our swords, cutting off an ear of anyone
who presumes to use violence against You. Rather, You would

have us make use of the sword of the Spirit (Cf. Eph. 6: 17) and begin Your conquest with the conquest of ourselves. May your kingdom triumph on earth as it is forever triumphant in heaven!

The Lord of hosts is with us; our stronghold is the God of Jacob.

O Lord and Leader of all armies, You are with us ... not as some remote official giving orders to be executed with military precision, but as an intimate friend to Whom as creatures we belong. We can rely on You with perfect trust and confidence. You are the God who protected Jacob in all his trials, although You challenged his mettle by an all-night struggle. You are the eternal Father Who will guide all His posterity.

Glory be to the Father.

Glory be to the Father, our refuge and strength, omnipotent Creator and Sustainer of all things ... and to the Son, our divine Saviour and Helper in tribulations, through Whom and with Whom we can offer an infinite sacrifice in atonement for our sins ... and to the Holy Ghost, the Paraclete and Sanctifier, Who helps us to profit by every opportunity to honor God and gain heavenly merit for ourselves. May this hymn of praise of God be multiplied by all the angels and saints in heaven, and thus please the Persons of the most holy Trinity forever and ever. Amen.

ANTIPHON: *God will help her with His countenance; God is in the midst of her, she shall not be moved.*

O holy Mother of God, so closely associated with Him always, keep me ever conscious of the divine indwelling in my soul!

ANTIPHON: *A habitation is in thee.*

Our Lady, Cause of our joy! Since your *fiat* made it possible for us to win the joys of Redemption, pray for us that we may win eternal joys!

PSALM 86

His foundation upon the holy mountains the Lord loves: the gates of Sion, more than any dwelling of Jacob.

The foundations of Jerusalem, city of peace and center of Hebrew worship, are in the holy mountains, O Lord ... that is, on the supernatural elevation of faith in You, the one true God. You love the gates of Sion above all the tabernacles of Israel. As the religious and political capital of the Jews, its history is typical of the struggles of the chosen people to preserve the true faith, to observe Your law, to keep Your covenant, to defend the Ark of the Covenant against any profanation, to offer sacrificial worship, and to adorn and embellish the temple as a sign of their profound reverence for You, O Jahweh, the most High!

Glorious things are said of thee, O city of God!

Yes, O Jerusalem, your glory has been great . . . so great that you are called the celestial city, the kingdom of God . . . but, O City of David, you were destined for greater glory: as the scene of the Passion and the Resurrection of One born of the royal line of David . . . the scene of the perfect holocaust of our High Priest, Jesus Christ, the Saviour and Redeemer of all mankind! Thus, you typify the universal Church established by Him. True, this "Cornerstone which the builders rejected" (Matt. 21: 42) wept over you, because, O City of Peace, you did not know the things that were for your peace. Nevertheless, you remain as a permanent lesson to all people who are favored by God, to be vigilant and prepared for His visitation, to regulate their lives by essential spiritual values, lest they suffer the fate of your utter destruction.

I tell of Egypt and Babylon among those that know the Lord . . .

O Lord, in spite of man's repeated failures, in spite of his ingratitude and indifference, You do not limit Your graciousness and goodness. You are mindful of Egypt and Babylon, of heathen nations of the Gentile world, even though Your chosen people have been untrue to You. Through Your indulgence the sinful woman won merciful pardon (John 8: 11) and the good thief made his criminal escape into heaven (Luke 23: 43). In an age of bewilderment and confusion, serious seekers of truth find their way by Your grace into Your Church. Let me not be too comfortably complacent about my faith, Lord, but let me show my appreciation for this gift by an ever more generous cooperation with Your grace. Let me pray daily for those outside the fold, for the missions, foreign and domestic, as well as for all the faithful, that they may profit by their heavenly heritage.

of Philistia, Tyre, Ethiopia: "This man was born there."

Souls of every race and nation ... souls of every economic and cultural and social level ... are to be saved for You, O Jesus! Just as all the foreign traders and travellers came to Jerusalem, they mingle today with the members of the faithful. They come in contact with Your Mystical Body. Is it not our duty, as members of Your Mystical Body, to lead them to know You, Jesus Christ, through our words and example? Is it not our duty to pray for them? As we sit in the bus or train, our Lord, let us not stare vacantly out the window or brood over some imagined slight. Instead, let us pray that the knowledge of You may come to all those riding in the same car ... to all those in the buildings we pass ... to those on the street ... to laborers, tradesmen, travellers ... to clerks and secretaries ... to all children and teachers in schools ... to their parents at home ... to children who will be born today ... to all professional men and women ... to scholars and writers ... to all engrossed in government or business ... to all the sick ... to the dying ... to the unemployed, the discouraged ... to all those whose names appear in newspapers ... to those heard on the radio ... to those on television ... to all the members of our fighting forces, on land or sea, or in the sky.

And of Sion they shall say: "One and all were born in her; and He who has established her is the Most High Lord."

Scattered throughout all nations are those who can claim spiritual descent from Jerusalem, the religious center preserving faith in You, the one, true God. May You guide all the heirs of Abraham to a recognition of the function and fulfillment of the Old Law given to Your chosen people. O eternal Father, may You bring them to a profound conviction of the mission of Your divine Son! Under the New Dispensation, O Jesus, You sent Your Apostles to teach all nations. You founded Your Church on the democratic principle which disregards linguistic, ethnic, nationalistic, political, economic and social barriers. Transcending all earthly ideals of freedom, You lead Your followers along the way of everlasting liberty ... the liberty known only to the children of God.

They shall note, when the peoples are enrolled: "This man was born there."

In the record of the last judgment, all members of the true faith and their leaders will be recognized by You, O God, and rewarded accordingly. At the commemoration of the living during the Holy Sacrifice of the Mass, during our short visits to the Blessed Sacrament, or as we say our OFFICE or night prayers, we specify our intentions, supplicating You for all the faithful, that they may become more devout . . . for all devout members of the Church, that they may grow and develop spiritually . . . for priests, brothers, and sisters, that they may increase in holiness . . . for all "our own," our relatives, friends, and benefactors, that they may reach high sanctity . . . for all members of our religious community and for all those served by them, that they may more generously love and glorify You . . . for the welfare of all those who make life happier through observance of the little courtesies, the smile, the generous gesture, the charity that is truly catholic. We must pray especially, too, for our spiritual leaders, for our Holy Father and all his intentions . . . our bishops, pastors and religious superiors, that they may successfully guide the flock committed to their care, spread Your kingdom on earth, and increase steadily in Christian holiness and zeal for the promotion of Your greater glory.

And all shall sing, in their festive dance: "My home is within thee."

Dwelling in Your holy city, O God, makes us desire to sing with happiness, according to the measure of our faith, the virility of our hope and the degree of our charity. Reason tells us that perfect happiness is the complete satiation of our intellect and will in their proper objects, truth and goodness. Therefore, O God, the highest truth accessible through faith should make us rejoice even in this life, if our wills strive correspondingly towards the attainment of goodness. As we come to know You better, our joy is intensified, O God, by the guarantee that complete happiness can be possessed by Your grace in our heavenly home, in the eternal contemplation of the Beatific Vision . . . where we shall gaze directly on You, the divine Essence of perfect truth . . . the divine Essence of absolute goodness!

Glory be to the Father.

Glory be to the Father, Whose providence arranged for the preservation of the faith in the one, true God, throughout all the ages of human history! Glory be to the Son, Who fulfilled the divine promises of the Old Law and through His merits and sufferings opened to all men the gates of heaven, closed against the human race since the commission of original sin! Glory be to the Holy Ghost, Who makes the Church infallible by His abiding presence, and provides its individual members with the means and the manner of their sanctification! As it was in the beginning, when the mind of God destined us for happiness . . .

and is now, when He gives the means to attain happiness . . . may His glory ever be the sole object of our eternal happiness! Amen.

ANTIPHON: *A habitation is in thee, as it were of us all who rejoice, O holy Mother of God.*

O Mary, Ark of the covenant! Tower of David! House of gold! Protect us, your children dwelling within the true Church of Christ. Help us to persevere steadfastly in the faith, to rejoice continually in its blessings, to lead others to it by our prayer and example, and finally, to be admitted into the everlasting habitation prepared for us in heaven!

THIRD NOCTURN

ANTIPHON: *Rejoice, O Virgin Mary.*

Rejoice, O Virgin Mary, and teach us to praise the Lord constantly by the purity of our lives, the submission of our intellects to truth, the resignation of our wills to divine wisdom.

PSALM 95

SING *to the Lord a new song; sing to the Lord, all ye lands.*

Sing, to express the exuberant joy that fills your hearts, all you who meditate on the meaning of our salvation! Less important triumphs elate us, win our enthusiastic praise. If our favorite team wins an athletic contest, our political candidate wins an election, if a business or professional project is successful, if our own work brings satisfaction, our hearts sing with delight, no matter how questionable the quality of our voices. Yet our eternal salvation is infinitely more important than any petty temporal triumph. Moreover, we who have been born after the coming of our Lord, can sing a new song, since the old forms of ancient worship have been supplanted by the perfect oblation of the Redeemer of all mankind. O eternal Father, all the earth should rejoice with us at the glad tidings of the Gospel, since Your divine Son has come into the world to save all men. At Christmas and at Easter, when people pause to consider the significance of the Incarnation and Redemption, they are much happier than usual; but later, burdened by temporal cares, they forget Your importance in their lives. Religious, who dedicate their lives to the cause of Christ, Your Son, should consider it a duty to keep alive all year the spirit of Christmas and Easter. Indeed, O God, the year is not long enough to meditate on the beneficial effects of these events on earth. Such meditating will bring us perpetual joy . . . a joy at once energetic and diffusive, to be spread among all members of human society in Your name.

Sing to the Lord; bless His name; announce His salvation, day after day.

Utter the praises of the Lord joyously! Spread the glad tidings of the Gospel by your very happiness! O souls who aspire to holiness, do not allow the demon of self-pity to make you pose as martyrs, magnifying sadly the size of your trifling sacrifices! The genuine martyrs were joyous, optimistic, detached from their sufferings, because they were saints who put into practice the teaching of Christ.

Singing Your praises, O Lord, suggests the blending of tones and the resultant harmony characteristic of members of the Mystical Body of Christ; it presupposes the exclusion of envy or jealousy, ostentation, vanity, or any other vice that would mar the perfection of the total offering of our talents to You . . . an offering which must be lived daily, if it is to reflect the stability of true love of You.

Tell His glory among the nations; among all peoples, His wondrous deeds.

Our modern era enjoys a remarkable system of rapid communication, so that news can be broadcasted around the world in a matter of seconds. How Saint Paul or Saint Francis Xavier would have revelled at such an opportunity, O God, to preach the biggest news on earth . . . the news of Your Gospel! If we are not missionaries in fact, O God, we want to be missionaries in spirit, spreading the light of the Gospel by the ardor and intensity of our prayers . . . by the television of good example. Our catholic hearts earnestly beseech Your Holy Spirit daily to effect the conversion of all peoples, all races and nations, of all souls everywhere on the globe.

For great is the Lord and highly to be praised; awesome is He, beyond all gods.

Records of unusual power, goodness, purity, courage, generosity, wisdom, honesty, beneficence, love . . . always excite admiration. But, O Lord, You possess all these attributes and a great many more, infinite in extent . . . unfathomable to human intelligence. However, in proportion to our knowledge of You, we desire to render You adequate praise, even though adequate praise would be infinite, and hence, beyond human ability. As we meditate on the luminous facets of Your reflected glory, our emotions vary amidst wonder, joy, admiration, awe, and reverential fear ... for You are formidable in Your power, O most mighty One, and far above all objects of idolatry set up by the human imagination. Contemplating Your supreme worth, our hearts burst forth into canticles of adoration and praise.

For all the gods of the nations are things of naught, but the Lord made the heavens.

All the gods of the Gentiles are false, because they are man's dreams of supermen, to satisfy his craving for solace and sympathy; however, these products of the imagination have no foundation in objective reality. Yet, Your personal, objective existence, O Lord, is evident from Your created works; for You have made the heavens, and all Your creations reveal Your knowledge, wisdom, and order, Your beauty, splendor, and power.

Splendor and majesty go before Him; praise and grandeur are in His sanctuary.

Whatever beauty and wisdom Your works reveal, O supreme and infinite Majesty, our personal knowledge of You is much more illuminating. To know You through the spiritual vision of faith is to love You ... to love You is to praise You ... but true praise of You is worthless, unless it leads to the holiness of service ... even to the point of heroic generosity in the sanctuary of Your abiding Presence.

Give to the Lord, ye families of nations, give to the Lord glory and praise; give to the Lord the glory due His name!

Break down prejudice which prevents the spread of truth, all you who wish sincerely for peace among nations! Seek the clear knowledge which culminates in praise! Render the glory, or "clear knowledge with praise"[1] which is due to the Creator and Redeemer of our life! Honor His name with reverence, all you countries of Gentiles, for you are the heirs of a glorious heritage, which can be won only through proper knowledge and love and service of the Lord.

---

1 St. Thomas, *Summa Theol.*, 2, 2, q. 103, a. 1, ad 3.

Bring gifts, and enter His courts; worship the Lord in holy attire.

Sacrifice and submission are exercises of faith, O all you souls outside the one, true fold! Sacrifice your prejudices and your opinions for certitude! Submit to the teaching of divine authority and eagerly pursue the truth in the Church established by Christ! There you will not be doubtful. There, you will have the opportunity and the satisfaction of adoring the Lord in liturgical worship, according to His desire and teaching. There, you will be assured of following the path of holiness pointed out by our supreme Exemplar.

Tremble before Him, all the earth; say among the nations: "The Lord is King."

May all the earth be stirred to profound reverence at the realization of Your infinite worth, O Lord! May all those who have not yet a personal acquaintance with You come to acknowledge You as their King! Truly have You spoken when You declared, "My kingdom is not of this world" (John 18: 36). Nevertheless, the interesting fact remains, that men cannot easily be indifferent to You, Lord. They will either love You or hate You. When they express their hatred of You, it is simply that they are trying to run away from You and from the obligations which they know in their hearts they owe You.

Yes, even though we act as rebels, we realize that You reign over us. When our actions are Christlike, You reign over our hearts. May we endeavor to make that reign more complete, in order to repair for our own periods of rebellion and for the perversity of all rebels.

He has made the world firm, not to be moved; He governs the peoples with equity.

In spite of the nebular hypothesis, O Lord, You have established the world, regulated by specific laws. Every true scientist admits that the physical laws governing the universe are constant and consistent in their operation. This fact is indicative of Your wisdom, O Lord and Creator. The moral law, too, founded on the divine, is constant and consistent and binding on all people. You, its divine Author, will judge all people according to it with equity.

Let the heavens be glad and the earth rejoice; let the sea and what fills it resound; let the plains be joyful and all that is in them!

Proper fulfillment of its purpose or destiny constitutes the perfection of Your created universe, O Lord. Hence, the heavens, the earth, the sea ... all render You extrinsic glory, as they cause our hearts to rejoice in You. In our atomic age, the very heavens seem glad, as we soar aloft through their pure atmosphere to a superterrestrial world. Here we see all things in a new perspective, where the colossal structures of earth are reduced by distance to very small points barely discernible in the picture lying below. Similarly, the movements of ocean waves carrying our ship can cause us quiet content; for, remote from the earth, we feel released from all cares connected with the crowded traffic of our lives. ... Here we experience again, O Lord, new confidence and trust in Your kindly providence.

As the scientist, O Lord, studies the microcosmic wonders of the earth revealed in laboratory analysis ... as the painter, poet, philosopher, or mystic contemplates the macrocosmic aspects of the universe, each one delights in his discovery of truth, or beauty, or love, reflecting Your divine genius. May the heavens, the sea, the earth and its produce thus communicate to all men the real secret of happiness which will lead them to You, O divine Truth, divine Beauty, divine Love!

Then shall all the trees of the forest exult before the Lord, for He comes; for He comes to rule the earth.

Trees, O heavenly Father, suggest the occasion of original sin ... yet they should cause men to rejoice: because Christ dignified by His Presence the barren tree of the Cross, whence He offered us the fruits of the Redemption. That we may be well prepared for the coming of Your Son, our Lord, at the last judgment, it is well to recall, too, His parable of the barren fig tree (Matt. 24: 32), as opposed to the one which yielded good fruit. If, by our vows, we are really nailed to the tree of the Cross, in imitation of Christ, then our sacrifices, through His merits, will yield their fruit in due season. Then shall all the trees of the woods rejoice before the Lord, because He comes to rule the earth.

He shall rule the world with justice and the peoples with His constancy.

According to the degree of our knowledge, O Lord, You will judge Your people. We may not feel so superior, then, to those not of the faith, for You will expect higher standards of conduct from all Your privileged friends. Hence, the quality and quantity of Your gifts, O Lord, make us very great debtors to You, Whom we must strive to imitate: for You will rule the world with justice and the peoples with Your constancy.

Glory be to the Father.

Glory be to the Father, Who created trees and their fruit for man to enjoy in the Garden of Paradise! Glory be to the Son, Who as a Child in the carpenter shop blessed with His touch the timber of trees, and exalted all trees by His Passion and Death on the Cross, raising them from a symbol of shame to a sign of conquest! Glory be to the Holy Ghost, Who guides men away from the noxious fungi of sin, and leads them to gaze upon the tree of the Cross and to relish the fruits of sanctification and salvation! As it was in the beginning, is now, and ever shall be, eternally. Amen.

ANTIPHON: *Rejoice, O Virgin Mary, thou alone hast destroyed all heresies in the whole world.*

Rejoice, O Virgin Mary, for you alone by your humble *fiat* have given the key for the solution of all heresies in the whole world, since you received so graciously the Angel announcing the message of divine Truth!

ANTIPHON: *Vouchsafe.*

Show us, O Mary, how we may praise the Lord in deed and in truth . . . that we may deserve not the condemnation of the Pharisee who entered the temple to pray but was so filled with pride that he spent his time praising himself.

PSALM 96

𝒯HE *Lord is King; let the earth rejoice; let the many isles be glad.*

O Lord and Master of the universe! You have dominion over all Your created works: whether or not all men have the spiritual vision to acknowledge You as their King, Your physical laws prevail. Moreover, Your truth prevails and Your moral law prevails. Consequently, the earth should rejoice; for, if human power could destroy it, the earth would become a mere shambles. No opposition to Your law, O God, can render it invalid. Our First Parents did not lessen Your royal power, but proved it in their subsequent punishment. Sins committed since the Fall have not lessened Your divine power. Therefore, since You have reigned from the very beginning of creation, let the earth rejoice!

Let many islands be glad, O Lord! An island represents a
safe harbor in a sea of peril. Detached and remote from the
mainland, it requires its inhabitants to have sturdy faith in
You and firm confidence in Your never failing providence. It
also offers abundant opportunity for solitude and reflection. Its
limited supplies require industry . . . a certain degree of asceti-
cism . . . and a healthy disregard of social conventions. Spiritual
persons, O Lord, resemble islands somewhat. Far removed from
the busy marts, they enjoy a degree of solitude and leisure to
commune with You . . . yet they offer peaceful welcome and
solace to travellers in this troubled sea of life. Buffeted and
lashed by raging storms, they appear tranquil after every tem-
pest, for they have developed an inner calm, a fortitude and
faith in You which renders them well-nigh impregnable. Let
many islands such as these be glad! Their social and economic
status is determined by an accumulation of divine treasures and
You are their sole sovereign, O King of kings!

*Clouds and darkness are round about Him, justice and judg-
ment are the foundation of His throne.*

Clouds of deep mystery surround You, O infinite Majesty,
impenetrable to finite intelligence. Purity of faith prepares
our souls for firm and intimate friendship with You, the Ineffable. As justice and rectitude are the foundations of Your
throne, so the cardinal virtues, including justice, form the solid
basis for the development of Christian perfection. May our
souls practice and perfect these virtues, that we may make
progress in the spiritual life.

Fire goes before Him and consumes His foes round about.

The fire which purifies shall go before You, O God of justice!
If the ardor of love is insufficient, the purifying fire of penance
or punishment must refine and cleanse souls of all dross. Your
punitive justice makes spiritually suicidal the smoldering passions of the wicked . . . while obdurate sinners are as ashes,
rarely re-enkindled to life.

*His lightnings illumine the world; the earth sees and trem-
bles.*

Few natural phenomena are more terrifying than flashes of
lightning and crashes of thunder. Through faith, however, Your
comforting hand, O heavenly Father, transforms fear into love.
The earth trembles from the sudden shocks of the storm; but
the spiritual man sees new causes for reverence and awe, as he
contemplates Your omnipotent power in action.

The mountains melt like wax before the Lord, before the Lord of all the earth.

Steep hills swiftly change into gentle slopes, as we speed along in a high-powered car. Mountains melt into insignificance, as our plane gains altitude and momentum. Similarly, in the realm of the supernatural, mountains melt as wax below the wings of the spirit. Before Your Face, that is, for one resigned to Your will, O God, momentous problems, looming as mountains on the horizon, melt as wax. Indeed, when one contemplates You, O Essence of infinite perfection, all the peaks of earthly power and achievement melt as wax which the sun has softened.

The heavens proclaim His justice, and all peoples see His glory.

O eternal Father! No matter how rich or poor, brilliant or stupid, old or young, healthy or handicapped, all men can enjoy the air, light, heat, beauty of the heavens and Your divine artistry in nature. These are commodities most valuable and most comforting to human life ... commodities over which can be exercised no human monopoly. When it rains, or hails, or snows in a certain district, all people within that area are affected by the elements. The sun shines indiscriminately and the wind blows on all classes of society. The rainbow thrills every heart. The starry wonders of the night can be contemplated by all persons. The variegated mountain scenery, the vastness of ocean or plain, present to every man the reflection of Your glory. This makes us rejoice, as we sing with the Psalmist: "The heavens proclaim His justice, and all peoples see His glory."

All who worship graven things are put to shame, who glory in the things of naught; all gods are prostrate before Him.

"You have made us for Yourself, O Lord!"[1] No human or subhuman object of worship can satisfy us. When men set up human fabrications as their idols, they not only blaspheme, but they are working for their own spiritual destruction. When they glory in their riches, or popularity, or power, or any other colossal ambition of their pride, they are usurping Your divine rights and, as Your enemies, they deserve utter ruin.

---

1 *Confessions of St. Augustine*, ed. by J. M. Campbell and M. R. P. McGuire (N. Y., Prentice-Hall, 1931), I, 1.

Surprisingly enough, examination of our own prayer may reveal no little idolatry: we waste so much incense on ourselves, when we think we are glorifying You, O God! As Pharisees of old we glory in our presence in the chapel, when others are not there; we may even glory in so many vain imaginings ... in the way we say the prayers ... the way we recite THE OFFICE; we glory in our regularity, our punctuality, our posture ... our pronunciation, our enunciation, or our rich, melodious tones! We fret at all the other pious worshippers ... they mispronounce the words and chant off key! The chapel gets too warm or cold for comfort. We grow resentful and our nerves are all on edge! In this self-centered state, dear Lord, we wonder that we ever pray at all. We beg You to grant us purity of prayer ... that we may learn to adore in spirit and in truth, and not in mere formulas or empty words.

Sion hears and is glad, and the cities of Juda rejoice because of Thy judgments, O Lord.

Persons who dwell in Your city, O God, should be men of strong faith ... scornful of self and sensitive to supernatural issues. Perceiving Your beauty and goodness and love, they should rejoice and adore You in earnest. In contrast to modern intellectuals, too self-sufficient to recognize Your personal existence, the cities of Juda, enlightened by faith, rejoiced in Your truth and exulted in Your judgments, O Lord! We humbly thank You for this great gift of faith! May it raise us above the horizons of selfish rationalism ... to love and adore truly Your eternal Reality!

Because Thou, O Lord, art the Most High over all the earth, exalted far above all gods.

For, O Lord, You are not a mere product of thought, constructed as a hypothesis, for the comfort of distressed humanity. You are higher than all earthly reaches ... exalted beyond all nature. You are perceived essentially in the realm of the supernatural. When a person descends from the supernatural plane, he begins to worship counterfeit gods. Only when one breathes in the pure atmosphere of faith, does he learn to love Your goodness and truth.

The Lord loves those that hate evil; He guards the lives of His faithful ones; from the hand of the wicked He delivers them.

"If thou lovest Me, keep My commandments" (John 14: 15), are Your words, O Lord. Yes, You said also, "No man can serve two masters" (Matt. 6: 24). Genuine love of You requires hatred of Your enemies, hatred of all evil. It is quite human to attempt a compromise with evil. We often find ourselves in the position of Pilate. We often succumb to evil simply for some slight temporal advantage. Help us, O Master, to be more courageously Christian. You guard the lives of Your faithful ones; from the wicked You deliver them. Keep us, dear Lord, from being weak today! Let us at least be courageous in some small thing! Deliver us from evil, dear Lord! Make us heroic, make us saints!

Light dawns for the just; and gladness, for the upright of heart.

O eternal Truth, You will enlighten all sincere seekers of truth. Joy will gladden those who strive to be good. You will never fail to reward all valiant efforts. Unswerving loyalty to You, heroic conduct in the day-by-day struggle, will never go unobserved by You, O divine Omniscience!

Be glad in the Lord, ye just, and give thanks to His holy name.

All you who strive to keep your hearts pure must rejoice in the blessing of the friendship of God. May you supplement purity of conscience with purity of praise. Let not vanity vitiate the adoration which belongs totally to the Lord!

Glory be to the Father.

Improve the quality of our faith, O Lord, increase the intensity of our hope and the ardor of our charity . . . that we may gain steadily a greater capacity for glorifying You in Your most holy Trinity!

ANTIPHON: *Vouchsafe that I may praise thee, O sacred Virgin; give me strength against thine enemies.*

O holy Virgin, may I praise you through the imitation of your virtues. Thus armored with your faith and trust, your humility and obedience and love, may I combat successfully the demon of pride.

ANTIPHON: *The angel of the Lord.*

O blessed Lady! Greatly do we rejoice when we reflect on the unique blessing the message of the Angel Gabriel brought to earth!

PSALM 97

Sɪɴɢ *to the Lord a new song, for He has done wondrous deeds.*

Sing canticles of praise to the Lord ... not simply as the Psalmist of old, who saw in prophetic vision the good things to be hoped for ... but sing hymns of gratitude for the fulfillment of man's highest hope! Because He has done wonderful things ... wonderful things for me personally ... wonderful things for my relatives and friends ... for my Sisters in religion ... for the entire congregation of Christians! He is willing to do still more wonderful things for all those who will allow Him.

His right hand has won victory for Him, His holy arm.

Most significant among these wondrous deeds is our Redemption wrought by You, O Lord and Saviour Jesus Christ, Who sits at the right hand of the Father! Through Your infinite merits and Your infinite love for us, our salvation was effected. Marvelous too, is the fact that the Church and the Sacraments established by You enable all men to benefit personally from the Redemption ... every single day of their lives!

The Lord has made His salvation known: in the sight of the nations He has revealed His justice.

Marvelous is the manner in which Your Gospel has spread, O Jesus! Your Church has developed and is steadily growing throughout the world ... in spite of persecutions, heresies, schisms, and regrettable individual lapses. Marvelous is the integrity of Your doctrine as it comes down to us through the centuries! Marvelous is the experience of every convert who embraces the teaching of the Church! Not restricting Your truth to the chosen people, O Jesus, You have demonstrated divine justice to the entire world by Your Crucifixion and Death, which indicate the awful price of sin.

He has remembered His kindness and His faithfulness toward the house of Israel.

Even to those who have rejected You, O Lord, You extend Your mercy and Your immutable truth. Repeatedly, You offer pardon to us, in spite of our innumerable offenses. Instead of punishing us for our malicious conduct, You plead with us and inspire us with renewed faith and courage to persevere in the path of perfection, no matter how many times we fail.

All the ends of the earth have seen the salvation by our God.

"Go ye into the whole world, and preach the gospel to every creature" (Mark 16: 15). This was Your commission, O Lord, given to Your Apostles. Your light and Your truth have been carried to all parts of the earth. Of course, just as the sun illuminates all parts of the earth, yet some organisms do not thrive, so, many souls exposed to Your teaching fail to profit spiritually by the experience. The human will remains free to accept or reject You, O Saviour. Many graces will be offered this day, O Lord. Men are free to accept or reject them. Grant that they may use them for Your greater honor and glory! May all those who are to be recipients of Your gifts today take advantage of them for their own soul's salvation and the spread of Your kingdom on earth!

Sing joyfully to the Lord, all ye lands; break into song; sing praise.

There are different ways of expressing joy, O Lord, but probably the most natural is to utter exclamations of articulate praise. The thought of Your divine goodness ... to us and to all peoples ... makes us eager to communicate our happiness to all men ... makes us urge them to share in our hymns of gratitude. Thus, rising above our petty self-commiseration, we cry: "Sing joyfully to the Lord, all ye lands; break into song: sing praise."

Sing praise to the Lord with the harp, with the harp and melodious song. With trumpets and the sound of the horn sing joyfully before the King, the Lord.

Sing to the Lord, all the earth! Blend your song of glory with the polyphonic melody of musical instruments! Arrange your hymns in contrapuntal harmony to the music of the spheres! Sing all day long, and not only during hours of formal choir! Sing by your silence! Sing with every note heard in the whispering of voices, or the play of children, or the serious and sometimes monotonous rendition of the daily class recitation! Sing glory to God with every word of greeting, with every conversation, with every subject taught, with every task accomplished, every stitch sewed, every gadget used, every step taken! Sing for all the rest of the earth, for those who are too pessimistic to sing ... for those who are too apathetic ... for those who know not the secret of your song! Rejoice, and pray that they may soon learn this mystic secret!

*Let the sea and what fills it resound, the world and those
who dwell in it.*

O venerable virgin souls! Why wait for a silver, or golden,
or diamond jubilee! Be jubilant now! Be jubilant because you
share in the gifts of eternity! The Lord does not consider you
too young to admit you to His eternal Presence ... to give you
His eternal blessing! Let every drop of water ... every mole-
cule of earth ... every physical motion on the surface of the
earth and in the depths of the water ... be so many acts of joy
and gratitude to the Lord for all He has bestowed on you! May
every living thing, and every human being found on land or
ocean, join in the multiple praises of the Lord which you send
heavenward in your jubilation!

*Let the rivers clap their hands, the mountains shout with
them for joy before the Lord, for He comes, for He comes to
rule the earth.*

You have created us for joy, O Lord! All nature sings with
joy, as it fulfills its proper destiny. Rivers rush to wider
waters; mountains rise serene in their majestic splendor; birds
twitter; flowers bud and blossom; the study of physical and
biological phenomena is replete with the wonders of Your
creative power. You will come to judge the earth, as You once
judged the tree by its fruit. May souls made to Your image
and likeness ... souls created for a joyous supernatural destiny
... be not found wanting!

*He will rule the world with justice and the peoples with
equity.*

O supreme Ruler of heaven and earth! You will not require
the testimony of witnesses or the pleading of a defendant's
counsel. Your omniscience will clarify all complications, as
You will judge the earth according to strict principles of justice.
Each person is responsible for the talents he has ... for the
divine favors bestowed ... for the profit he has earned ... for
other souls he has influenced. O adorable Majesty, grant us
the grace now to correspond with all Your graces! May our
charity serve to win Your grace for others. May we now express our joy in prayerful Psalms and ardent works of praise,
that the final judgment may lead us to eternal bliss!

Glory be to the Father.

No matter what distractions we may suffer during other
prayers, O Lord, let not our attention lag as we sing the *Gloria.*
With filial reverence, let us adore You, O Father ... with

fervent desire, let us seek sacramental, sacrificial union with Your Son ... and ever strive towards the sanctification of our own souls and that of others, according to the inspirations of the Holy Ghost!

ANTIPHON: *The angel of the Lord declared unto Mary, and she conceived of the Holy Ghost, alleluia.*

O blessed Lady! Prepare our hearts to reap great spiritual profit by frequent and serious reflection on all the liturgy of Advent, that we may render joyous praise to the infant King.

VERSICLE: *Grace is poured forth on thy lips.* RESPONSE: *Therefore, God hath blessed thee forever.*

O Mary, whose every gesture of body, soul, mind, and heart spoke of the rich blessings of divine grace enjoyed by you, pray that we may act always in a manner worthy of the divine favors bestowed on us.

Our Father ... And lead us not into temptation. But deliver us from evil.

Our Father ... let us keep our hand confidently in Yours, as we journey along the paths of life. Let this continual handclasp be a sign of our faith ... a mark of our trust ... and a pledge of our everlasting intimacy! May Your paternal providence keep us, Your children, safe from all temptation and evil. Amen.

ABSOLUTION

By the prayers and merits of the blessed Mary ever Virgin and of all the Saints, may the Lord bring us to the kingdom of Heaven. Amen.

O Mary, Mediatrix of all graces! By your prayers and merits, and by the prayers and merits of all our patron saints and of all the unknown saints in heaven, may our Lord bring us to meditate effectively on His teaching, that we may one day enter His divine kingdom of heaven.

VERSICLE: *Pray, Lord, a blessing.*

BLESSING: *May the Virgin Mary with her loving Child bless us. Amen.*

In order to derive great spiritual profit from the lessons we
are about to read from the Book of Ecclesiasticus, we ask for a
special blessing. The response given by our religious superior
directs our attention to the Madonna, who holds her divine
Child up to bestow on us His precious blessing.

Ordinary Lessons During the Year

Lesson I: (Ecclus. 24, 11-13)

*In all things I sought rest, and I shall abide in the inheritance
of the Lord. Then the Creator of all things commanded and
said to me, and He that made me rested in my tabernacle; and
He said to me: Let thy dwelling be in Jacob, and thine inheritance in Israel, and take root in My elect.*

O divine Wisdom! You seek the rest and quiet of a soul that
is recollected . . . at peace with its neighbors . . . at peace with
its own conscience . . . a soul tranquil in its humility and self-
control. You desire to abide there where the Lord has bestowed
His richest heritage . . . in the soul possessing the gift of faith
and all its concomitant blessings. O supernatural Wisdom, declared in Sacred Scripture to be the greatest single attribute of
the divine Essence . . . in whom the Lord dwells as in His
tabernacle . . . You, obedient to His desire, have come to the
chosen people of God, to the race of Abraham and Isaac and
Jacob and to all the house of Israel, in order to lead them, in
spite of their vicissitudes, to preserve intact their faith in the
one, true God.

But Thou, O Lord, have mercy on us. Thanks be to God.

At the conclusion of each lesson, which contains a reflection
on the attribute of divine Wisdom, we humbly petition You,
O God, to have mercy on us, realizing full well that the Holy
Ghost has endowed us with the gratuitous gift of wisdom, by
which we can reap spiritual profit. As the choir responds *Deo
gratias*, we offer up our sentiments of gratitude for this gift of
the Holy Ghost and breathe a prayer that it may be increased
in ourselves and others.

Response: *O holy and immaculate virginity, I know not
with what praises to extol thee; because Him whom the
heavens could not contain, thou hast borne in thy womb.*

VERSICLE: *Blessed art thou among women, and blessed is the fruit of thy womb.* RESPONSE: *Because Him whom the heavens could not contain, thou hast borne in thy womb.*

O immaculate Virgin, inspired with a wisdom beyond every degree of human attainment, I know not how to praise you, who were found worthy to become the Mother of eternal Wisdom! Blessed are you among women, O Mary, Seat of Wisdom, and blessed is the Fruit of your womb. Because Him Whom the heavens could not contain, you have borne as Wisdom incarnate!

VERSICLE: *Pray, Lord, a blessing.*

BLESSING: *May the Virgin of Virgins herself,* possessing heavenly wisdom far beyond our comprehension, *intercede for us with the Lord. Amen.*

LESSON II   (Ecclus. 24, 15-16)

*A*ND *so I was established in Sion, and in the holy city likewise I rested, and my power was in Jerusalem. And I took root in an honorable people, and in the portion of my God His inheritance; and my abode is in the full assembly of saints.*

O Holy Spirit of Wisdom, You established in the hearts of the ancient Hebrews the faith in the true God and You guided His proper worship in the temple of Jerusalem on Mount Sion. You made fertile the virginal and immaculate flower of this honorable people, Mary, who by Your power conceived and brought forth Wisdom incarnate for the salvation of the world. You descended in person as the Paraclete promised by the risen Christ and You infallibly guide the Church and You are the delight of her saints forever!

RESPONSE: *Blessed art thou, O Virgin Mary, who* by the cooperation of the Spirit of Wisdom *hast borne the Lord, Creator of the world. Thou hast brought forth Him that made thee, and ever remainest* the wisest *virgin.*

VERSICLE: *Hail Mary, full of grace, the Lord is with thee.* RESPONSE: *Thou hast brought forth Him that made thee, and ever remainest a virgin* ... in fact, the purest and wisest of all virgins.

Glory be to the Father.

Glory be to the Father, the Essence of absolute Wisdom! Glory be to the Son, incarnate Wisdom! Glory be to the Holy Ghost, the divine Spirit of Wisdom! O Mary, Seat of Wisdom, you have brought forth Him Who made you, and you have ever remained the wisest of virgins.

VERSICLE: *Pray, Lord, a blessing.*

BLESSING: *May the Lord, through His Virgin Mother's intercession, grant us salvation and peace. Amen.*

LESSON III   (Ecclus. 24, 17-20)

I was exalted like a cedar in Libanus, and as a cypress tree on Mount Sion. I was exalted like a palm tree in Cades, and as a rose plant in Jericho. As a fair olive tree in the plains, and as a plane tree by the water in the streets was I exalted. I gave forth a sweet fragrance like cinnamon and aromatic balm. I yielded a sweetness of odor like the choicest myrrh.

O Holy Spirit of Wisdom, what abundant material for reflection has the inspired writer suggested in a comparatively few verses! As he evokes in rapid succession the images of tall, graceful trees, we admire more and more the exalted nature of Your beauty, Your solidity, Your loveliness and Your strength. The costly, rich, and beautiful cedars of Libanus, used to adorn the tabernacle of the Lord and the temple of Solomon, are symbols of Your supernatural treasures. Moreover, inasmuch as the height, straightness, and durability of these young trees made them useful for masts on ships, they symbolize Your perpetual guidance of Holy Mother Church (Cf. Ezech. 27: 5). The cedar described in Ezechiel (17: 22) is also a prophetic symbol of the Messias and His kingdom. The cool and refreshing breezes offered by the shade of the cypress trees of Mount Sion indicate the spiritual solace and comfort You give in Your office of Paraclete. The lofty branches of the graceful palm, flexible, yet sturdy enough to withstand any storm, and producing a hidden and delectable fruit, bespeak Your dignity and majesty and holiness (Cf. meaning of *Cades,* "holy"). They suggest the victory of wisdom over foolishness, Christ over sin, the Cross over human ambition.

The more humble trees, too, by a strange paradox, indicate the loftiness of Your virtue: the olive tree suggests Your peace,

Your soothing and strengthening power, the fruit of Your sacred Presence. The rose plant, significant of Your love, distills its drops of precious perfume even for the enjoyment of the blind, who cannot glimpse external beauty, but can profit by Your heavenly inspirations. It recalls to our minds, too, in its connection with Jericho, the parable of a certain Samaritan, going from Jerusalem to Jericho, who, by following Your inspiration, merits to be mentioned by our divine Saviour as a model of fraternal charity (Luke 10: 33). The plane tree, offering the plenitude of its shade near the water in the well-trafficked streets, shows us that You breathe where You will, and that Your coming is not simply to those exalted in positions of social or even spiritual authority.

The delicate aroma of cinnamon and balm and myrrh indicates the many differences in the manner and quality of Your inspirations, their soothing yet stimulating unction, their preservative power. By analogy to Your gift of wisdom, the myrrh undoubtedly refers to the resulting fragrance of the virtues of holy souls who, by the death of earthly desires, anoint their bodies and prepare them for burial.

As we contemplate the sensible beauty of these stately trees and fragrant plants, there is etched in our spirit the vision of another tree, severe, even forbidding, and stripped of all foliage and fruit, save the living and personal Fruit of divine Love. This is the tree of the Cross . . . the tree of Sacrifice . . . the tree of supernal Beauty in its spiritual significance. Its horizontal and vertical lines exemplify the great contrast between human and divine conceptions of wisdom. Worldly wisdom scoffs at the nonsense of the Cross. Omniscience proclaims the secret of its eternal worth. O Holy Spirit of God, have mercy on us and teach us truly to appreciate this secret of Your eternal wisdom! Teach us to contemplate frequently our divine Lord on His Cross and regulate our conduct by His standards of love!

Te Deum

We praise Thee, O God; we acknowledge Thee to be our Lord.[1]

As we repeat this magnificent prayer, we can scarcely remain unaffected by its contemplative spirit. The frequent recurrence of *Te, Tibi, Tu*, as the initial words in successive verses, keeps our attention focused continually on Your

---

1 Cf. Britt, *op. cit.*, pp. 14-16. See also THE LITTLE OFFICE (N. Y., Pustet, 1953), pp. 46-53.

adorable Majesty. Overshadowing all the admirable products of created matter . . . towering beyond the loftiest attainments and conceptions of human genius . . . the vertical beam of the Cross, rooted in the earth, yet infinite in its spiritual altitude, grandeur, beauty, and value, directs our attention to You. As we continue to look up and ponder on the mystic significance of the Cross for us, individually and collectively, profound sentiments of gratitude burst into song: "We praise Thee, O God; we acknowledge Thee to be our Lord."

All the earth doth worship Thee, the Father everlasting.

Organic and inorganic substances worship You, for they exist by Your creative power and follow faithfully Your universal laws; while human beings, even atheists, are dependent on Your creative and sustaining power. All, even perverse spirits, are subject to Your divine command.

To Thee all the angels cry aloud; the heavens and all the heavenly Powers. To Thee the Cherubim and Seraphim continually do cry: Holy, Holy, Holy, Lord God of hosts.

The exultant Trisagion which gives the signal for the most sacred and solemn part of Holy Mass, continues every moment of eternity, as the nine choirs of angels reverently adore in most intense worship the infinite perfection of Your Being.

Heaven and earth are full of the majesty of Thy glory.

It does not take the mind of a genius to discover the causality of creative splendor. It does take simple faith to recognize You as its supreme Cause, O almighty God, our All-good, All-wise, All-powerful, All-loving and All-merciful Father!

The glorious choir of the Apostles praise Thee. The admirable company of the Prophets praise Thee. The white-robed army of Martyrs praise Thee.

Peter, Andrew, James, John, Thomas, Matthew, Philip, Bartholomew, James the Less, Thaddeus, and Simon . . . venerable and true members of the original Apostolic College . . . whose unmitigated zeal for Your glory on earth is matched only by their absorption in You . . . are not simply names of historic record whose memory fades with the years. There they are, enjoying a more noble life, worshipping uninterruptedly before your throne, O divine Master, without any opposition, interference, or imperfection characteristic of their earthly struggles. There too, Isaias, Jeremias, Ezechiel, Daniel, Zacharias, Malachias, and all the other ancients who preached fearlessly the truth granted in prophetic vision, now contemplate forever Your profound mysteries, O ineffable Majesty!

Saints Stephen, Paul, and all the other glorious witnesses of the faith ... from the Holy Innocents down to our modern martyrs, victims of diabolical hatred ... have consecrated their lives on earth and the whole of eternity to Your worship.

The holy church throughout all the world acknowledges Thee, the Father of infinite majesty, Thine adorable, true, and only Son, also the Holy Ghost, the Comforter.

Holy Mother Church, whose edifices and altars are marked by the sign of the Cross and the symbol of Your most holy Trinity ... whose prayers begin and end with this most sacred symbol ... whose purpose is to promote Your glory and lead men to share in the fruits of the Redemption ... renders prayer and sacrifice and infinite praise to You every hour of the day in all parts of the world, through the merits of Your Son.

Thou art the King of Glory, O Christ!

Suddenly our gaze shifts back from the vertical to the transverse beam of the living Crucifix. There we consider the divine Victim riveted to the Cross, as an everlasting proof of our salvation. We see the arms of the eternal High Priest forever outstretched, as a gesture of supplication. We perceive, too, in this far-flung gesture of arms outstretched, the all-embracing charity of infinite Goodness, Who desires all men to profit by the Redemption. As we contemplate thus the divine Victim, the divine High Priest, the divine Charity, our lips proclaim: "Thou art the King of Glory, O Christ!" Yes, O Jesus, You are the King of Glory, because You alone of all men can possess the perfect knowledge of God the Father ... You alone, therefore, can render Him adequate love and sacrifice, reparation and praise. You alone, true God and true Man, can be the perfect Priest and Victim, the perfect Pontifex to bridge the abyss between matter and spirit, between the natural and supernatural worlds, between humanity and divinity, between time and eternity.

Thou art the everlasting Son of the Father.

Therefore, You have become our Brother and have raised us to the royalty of heirs of God, the Father. You have taught us to appreciate His paternal interest. You have taught us to pray to Him, and properly to adore Him.

When Thou didst take on Thyself to deliver man, Thou didst not disdain the Virgin's womb.

O Jesus, beloved Saviour, Your true greatness is shown in Your humility which, as Saint Paul explains, caused You, God, "to take the form of a servant, being made in the likeness of men, and in habit found as a man . . . becoming obedient unto death, even the death of the cross" (Philippians 2: 7-8).

Having overcome the sting of death, Thou didst open the kingdom of Heaven to all believers.

Death is irreparable and, from a natural point of view, the worst of all possible afflictions. It would leave beloved survivors inconsolable, were it not for the convictions offered by our holy faith. For, through You, O Christ, "the hope of a blessed resurrection hath shone upon us, that those whom the certainty of dying afflicteth, may be consoled by the promise of future immortality. For unto Thy faithful, O Lord, life is changed, not taken away; and the abode of this earthly sojourn being dissolved, an eternal dwelling is prepared in heaven" (Preface, Requiem Mass). You have saved us from eternal death, merited by our sins, O Lord! You have opened to believers the kingdom of heaven.

Thou sittest at the right hand of God, in the glory of the Father. We believe that Thou shalt come to be our Judge.

We believe, O Jesus, Master and Redeemer, that even as You came on earth to sanctify and save men, You will again execute the will of Your Father and come at last to judge men at the end of the world. We look upon You now with confidence, as a tender, loving Friend. May we clasp You then in an everlasting embrace of love, when You will pronounce our inevitable fate for all eternity!

We therefore pray Thee to help Thy servants, whom Thou hast redeemed with Thy precious blood.

O Lord, let not Your sacred Passion and Death have been in vain! Let not Your thirst for souls be unslaked! Let not Your love be ineffectual! Since one single drop of Your most precious blood could redeem the whole world, save Your servants for whom You shed Your blood so abundantly!

Make them to be numbered with Thy saints in glory everlasting.

While the primary purpose of one's life is Your extrinsic glory, dear Lord, personal sanctity and happiness are directly related to the degree to which one contributes to Your glory. Sanctify us even now, O Lord, so that we may live the life of grace and intimacy with You, which will be simply the beginning of the blessed state we hope to enjoy forever in heaven!

*Save Thy people, O Lord, and bless Thine inheritance.
Govern them and raise them up forever.*

Naturally, O Lord, we seek physical security, but supernaturally, we desire spiritual salvation. You have shown us,
by Your Passion and Death on the Cross, which is to be preferred. Let us never weaken, but be courageous enough to
imitate Your example. Graciously bless Your inheritance, O
Lord . . . bless Your heirs made so by Baptism . . . bless those
infants just receiving the gift of supernatural life, that it may
grow and develop and bring them to generous sanctity. Help
those souls who, having strayed from Your paths, have lost
sanctifying grace. Bring them back to Your friendship. Govern
them all and exalt them all, according to Your promise,
"And I, if I be lifted up, shall draw all things unto Me"
(John 12: 32).

*Every day we bless Thee. And we praise Thy name forever,
yea, forever and ever.*

All day, every day, at every single moment of the day, we
desire to worship You with all our power and strength, to love
You with the total capacity of our being, to praise You with
the greatest intensity of our energy, O most divine Majesty!
May this glorious privilege allowed us in time, increase in
effect and in power for all eternity!

Vouchsafe, O Lord, this day to keep us without sin.

Teach us, O Lord, to praise You not in words alone and in
desires, but in deed and in truth. Help us to keep this day
without sin, and to make definite progress in the spread of
Your kingdom and in the serious cultivation of virtues pleasing
to You.

*Have mercy on us, O Lord, have mercy on us. Let Thy
mercy, O Lord, be upon us, as we have hoped in Thee.*

O Lord, we hail You as Master, King, and Judge, but also as
Lover, Redeemer, Saviour, and Spouse! We admire Your truth
and Your justice, but we need Your goodness and mercy above
all Your favors. Have mercy on us, O Lord, Your children,
according to Your most tender and abundant mercy. Surely
our trust in You could never exceed Your merciful goodness!

In Thee, O Lord, I have hoped; let me never be confounded.

We have trusted greatly in Your mercy, O Lord! Let us not
be disappointed forever. As we reflect on Your infinite and
heroic love, shown for us personally on the Cross . . . and shown
for us every time the Holy Sacrifice of the Mass is offered . . .

we know that Your infinite love and power will be matched by Your infinite mercy. Conscious that Your Death on the Cross and Your subsequent burial formed but a prelude to Your glorious Resurrection, we dare to hope, too, for a blessed resurrection. As we look at our crucifix, we know that this hope will never be in vain.

III

LAUDS

𝒞ʜᴇ Angel Gabriel was sent.

O Mary! The divine intervention in human affairs is marked
by your heavenly visitor. More remarkable still is God's
personal concern for each one of us by the appointment of a
Guardian Angel. Only very important personages in this world
are accompanied by secret service men who act as protectors.
Our souls must be of very great value, since our Father in
heaven gives us His personal escorts. Angel Guardian, henceforth may I imitate the Blessed Virgin Mary by complete
docility to your direction.

Psalm 92

*𝒞ʜᴇ Lord is King, in splendor robed; robed is the Lord and
girt about with strength.*

Superior to all physical force, superior to all human power,
O Lord, You rule over all creation. But the magnificence of
Your power and the beauty and strength of Your truth are not
confined to the sensible order. Hearts belonging to You discern and appreciate, through eyes of faith, Your spiritual power
and beauty and strength, O infinitely perfect Being! Of course,
men of prayer are concerned about human welfare: they ask

for Your assistance in gaining their "daily bread." But they strive to obtain Your spiritual gifts, even though this means the renunciation of human pleasures. Scoffers claim religion is an escape from reality . . . an attempt to solve life's problems by wishful thinking . . . yet the believer faces the total reality, not limited to material phenomena. The power, beauty, wealth, and strength he esteems are principally in the realm of grace. When he praises You, O Lord, he is conscious that he is praising One Who claimed: "My kingdom is not of this world" (John 18: 36).

And He has made the world firm, not to be moved.

In these days, O Lord, many good people worry about atom bombs and the end of the world; for experts have developed high-powered explosives in their attempt to discover more about matter. Earthly rulers who act through expediency . . . earthly thinkers who plan for material progress only . . . must logically work for the destruction of opposing forces. But You Who created the world from nothing . . . You Who sustained it for all these centuries . . . will not allow its annihilation without Your consent. Are we of such little faith that we cannot trust You?

Thy throne stands firm from of old; from everlasting Thou art, O Lord.

The harm done by human beings can affect only temporal conditions, if only we remain united to You Who are eternal, O Lord! The harm done by evil powers in the realm of the intellectual and spiritual order can be irreparable, only if we abandon our faith and hope and love of You, O Lord!

The floods lift up, O Lord, the floods lift up their voice; the floods lift up their tumult.

O Jesus! In the stream of time we suffer many storms, even violent ones, which jeopardize the earthen craft of our humanity. But You can command the waves to be still. Nero's attempt to crush the Church failed; English efforts to stamp out the Church failed; Communistic wholesale slaughters are no more successful. The sneering innuendoes of faithless critics only serve to strengthen our ardor for the truth. Your Crucifixion, O Truth incarnate, prepared the way for Your glorious Resurrection and our Redemption!

Totalitarian rulers may roar; many may lift up their voices against Your Holy Church; Kant and Hegel and Nietzsche, Descartes and Taine, James and Dewey, and a host of modern professors have caused chaos by their floods of eloquent but erroneous teaching. We need not lose heart, O Lord! Opposing their scepticism is the strong bulwark of our faith.

More powerful than the roar of many waters, more powerful than the breakers of the sea: powerful on high is the Lord.

Admirable are the achievements of science, atomic force, and the tremendous possibilities of matter. Far more admirable are You, O uncreated Power, Who sustains all being and keeps it under Your divine control.

Thy decrees are worthy of trust indeed; holiness befits Thy house, O Lord, for length of days.

Cardinal Mindszenty, Cardinal Stepinac, Cardinal Wyszynski, Archbishop Beran, Bishop Ford, and Your faithful witnesses persecuted for their devotion to the faith would not exchange Your eternal truth for all the material power, knowledge, and comfort in the world. They have preferred to give up their lives rather than forfeit Your eternal truth; for they recognize that Your testimonies are exceedingly credible, O Lord, and they are firmly convinced of their absolute value. Therefore, holiness becomes Your house ... that is, living on this earth of Yours according to the principles we profess, is essential, O Lord. What else matters? Holiness becomes our convent home, O Lord, for there You abide under the same roof with us ... holiness becomes the temple of our souls, O Lord, for You are with us always while we remain in the state of grace!

Glory be to the Father.

Glory be to the Father, the Creator and cause of our faith! Glory be to the Son, the Saviour and pledge of our hope! Glory be to the Holy Ghost, the Inspirer of our love and Sanctifier of our praise and service of the Lord!

ANTIPHON: *The Angel Gabriel was sent to Mary, a Virgin espoused to Joseph.*

O admirable Saint Joseph, who, without knowing the intimate secret communicated by the Angel to Mary, still persisted in loving faith and trust in God, pray that we may increase daily in faith and hope. and practice ardent charity towaras God and our fellow men.

ANTIPHON: *Hail Mary.*

Hail Mary, immaculate Mother, full of grace! Pray that we may daily grow in grace and keep close to the divine Source of grace!

PSALM 99

SING *joyfully to the Lord, all ye lands; serve the Lord with gladness.*

Rejoice, all you people on earth ... rejoice in the divine royalty of your origin. Reflect that if it is good to be alive, you enjoy life because almighty God has chosen to create you out of many millions of possible beings. Consider that if the circumstances of life are rather adverse at certain times, you have been placed here because of the almighty Father's personal interest in you ... He has given you opportunities to prove your mettle ... to increase your merit. Accept the challenge gladly, in order to show your courage and fidelity to the sovereign Master and King.

Come before Him with joyful song.

Naturally, when we come into Your eucharistic Presence, we are filled with joy in proportion to our personal love for You, O Jesus! Our love is indeed very great, and certainly exceeds our power of expression. The liturgy provides the means for uttering that love in a joyous ... a reverently joyous manner. Help us enter into its spirit, especially in our chanting of the Psalms of THE OFFICE with a reverent feeling of interior joy. If we have a choice between saying THE OFFICE privately or in choir, let us remember Your words, O divine Lord: "Wherever two or three are gathered together in My name, there I am in the midst of them" (Matt. 18: 20). Let us enter into Your sight joyously.

Know that the Lord is God; He made us, His we are; His people, the flock He tends.

O Lord, You have personally created our individual souls. You have breathed each soul into a body especially prepared for it ... surrounded us with every possible attention and comfort and advantage, even from the moment of birth ... through the helplessness of infancy, and the problematic period of youth. Your constant concern for us continues with the years. Hence, we cannot be indifferent to You, to Whom we owe our very lives and sustenance. We pray humbly to You, dear Father in heaven, to keep us from ever being so proud and self-sufficient as to neglect the love and gratitude we owe to You. We are

Your people, and the sheep of Your pasture. We belong to You, our Creator. Moreover, we have been made Your children and heirs in a particular way by the gift of Baptism. We are Your sheep, O divine Shepherd, Who gave Your life for Your sheep.

Enter His gates with thanksgiving, His courts with praise; give thanks to Him; bless His name.

Therefore, we enter into Your temple, thanking You for the gifts of life ... but more particularly for the gifts of the spiritual life ... the gifts of faith and Redemption. We thank You for the vocation that is ours in being chosen to come here and sing Your praises. Let us enter Your courts with hymns. Help us to enter the spirit of the liturgical ceremony, reverently joyous, and humbly grateful for all Your graces and blessings. We confess to You ... acknowledging Your sovereign power over us ... not so much to bring it to Your attention, but so that we shall never forget ... and the world so proud of modern progress will never forget ... the worship and love, the esteem and gratitude we owe to You, our Creator and Redeemer. We want to praise Your name ... not merely in the words of the Psalms, uttered by the lips ... but with the full correspondence of the mind ... with the love and desire springing from the heart.

For He is good: the Lord, Whose kindness endures forever, and His faithfulness to all generations.

Truly, O Lord, You are good: a relish for Your spiritual delights is a gift of the Holy Ghost, eagerly to be sought and cultivated. Your kindness continues forever, since there is no limit to Your spiritual treasure, or to Your benign goodness in heaping favors upon us. Your truth is bestowed on all generations. The gift of faith, which You have so gratuitously bestowed on us ... that we might know the truth and thus know You ... has been imparted to many generations of people. It will still be given to many other generations. We pray for those who have it ... that they may profit by it and lead others to seek it. We pray for those who have it not ... that they may be inspired to receive it and cooperate with the grace it will bring. We thank you, Lord, in humble gratitude for all the blessings and all the happiness we have received during life, because we are members of the one, true faith.

Glory be to the Father.

Glory be to the Father, Who has created us for the highest spiritual joy! Glory be to the Son, Who has brought us the

Sacraments which lead to that joy! Glory be to the Holy Spirit, Who inspires us with the love and desire of possessing forever the personal Cause of our joy!

ANTIPHON: *Hail, Mary, full of grace, the Lord is with thee; blessed art thou among women, alleluia.*

Hail, Mary, full of grace and channel of all God's graces to us! The Lord is with you and, therefore, you are blessed among women! Teach us to appreciate the divine Presence among us as the most precious gift of all His blessings . . . teach us sincere and unaffected and practical love for Him Who deigns to dwell among us. Alleluia! As we again anticipate the advent of the infant King, may our praise of Him resound in many exultant and joyous Alleluias!

ANTIPHON: *Fear not, Mary.*

Fear not, Mary, for the Lord, Source of all grace, is with you! Help me to appreciate more fully the wondrous graces He has brought to me through you!

PSALM 62

O God, Thou art my God Whom I seek.

O God, with the first rays of dawn my thoughts turn towards You. When against the morning sky I perceive the tall, cross-surmounted spire signalling a new day, my heart is immediately grateful to You for another opportunity to offer You better service. As You send the gradual but steady influx of light into a world of darkness, I think of the imperceptible but real influx of grace into souls spiritually blind, cold, lukewarm, or discouraged . . . perhaps into souls darkened by sin. Praying for this influx of grace into souls, I remember the gradual series of graces given to me personally. I look forward eagerly to You, O Source of grace, coming into my own soul this very morning . . . and into the souls of those near and dear to me.

For Thee my flesh pines and my soul thirsts like the earth, parched, lifeless and without water.

I realize that, with David, my flesh pines for You . . . my mind thirsts for a more intimate knowledge of You, O infinite Wisdom . . . my will thirsts for a closer and closer imitation of Your perfect charity . . . my weak humanity dares to aspire to an everlasting union with Your divinity. So intense is this thirst for You that my soul seems parched and lifeless without You. It becomes quite clear that the happiness for which You have made me will never be found in earthly delights, but only in You.

Thus have I gazed toward Thee in the sanctuary to see Thy power and Thy glory.

Therefore, I hasten to rise at the sound of the bell . . . to go before Your altar . . . to offer You my morning prayer. I gaze towards Your tabernacle, as I prepare for the contemplation of Your divine attributes . . . Your strength, transcending in quality all physical power . . . Your glory, surpassing in intensity every human conception. I adore You profoundly in the mystery of Calvary . . . the mystery which brings us so much of Your mercy.

For Thy kindness is a greater good than life; my lips shall glorify Thee.

Of all Your attributes, O Lord, Your divine mercy reflects most Your tender interest in mankind. If existence is a gift for which I should be grateful, how much more should I esteem the gifts of the supernatural life, made available through Your generous mercy. The corporal and spiritual favors of Your bounty have led me to know and love You and to realize that Your mercy is far above life itself. Hence, if I struggle so energetically to preserve life, how much more zealous should I be in defending the supernatural life . . . by corresponding with Your mercy and by promoting its effects wherever and whenever I can.

In imitation of You, O divine Redeemer, Who ransomed men from the slavery of sin, the members of the Order of Our Lady of Mercy used to offer their lives to ransom captive prisoners. Clearly, they understood that Your mercy is better than life. Consecrated to You as a Sister of Mercy, I also enjoy the inestimable privilege of sharing daily in the corporal and spiritual works of Your mercy . . . rescuing the poor from their distress, the sick from their affliction, and the ignorant from their captive state of darkness. Through these experiences, as a daughter of Mother McAuley, I learn that Your mercy is better than life. Therefore, my lips delight in praising You . . . I offer every power of my being to You!

Thus will I bless Thee while I live; lifting up my hands, I will call upon Thy name.

Thus, during my entire life I will bless You . . . in all the labors of the active life, dedicated to works of Your mercy . . .

and in all my prayers of adoration and thanksgiving as well.
And in Your name will I lift up my hands ... to give all I have
to You. Likewise, in all my supplications will I appeal to You
as a merciful Father to pour forth ever more abundant gifts of
Your infinite mercy upon Your poor, afflicted children.

*As with the riches of a banquet shall my soul be satisfied,
and with exultant lips my mouth shall praise Thee.*

At the spiritual feast of Your merciful kindness, let my soul
partake of the most delicious morsels, that my mouth shall
praise You with lips of joy. Let my relish for divine wisdom
be keen. Let a practical zeal for Your glory fill my entire being. Let me be an instrument helping others to know and love
and praise You, O Father of all goodness and mercy.

*I will remember Thee upon my couch, and through the night
watches I will meditate on Thee.*

Let my last prayer at night be Yours, O Lord: "Into Thy
hands I commend my spirit" (Luke 23: 46). During sleepless
periods let me recall that faithful contemplatives arise to bless
You through the canonical hours of the night watches. I pray
that they may offer You pure prayer. I also offer my own
fitful periods of wakefulness for those who toss on beds of pain
and cannot sleep ... for those whom mental torture keeps
awake ... for those who spend their nights in moral dangers.
Let the labors of the active life, which interfere with a continual state of reflection on divine truths, be dedicated always
to You. In moments of leisure, let my mind turn habitually
to You, so that my meditation hours will be pleasing to You.

*That Thou art my help, and in the shadow of Thy wings I
shout for joy.*

Because You have been my helper, my prayers should not
be simply monologues recited *to* You, but intimate conversations
enjoyed *with* You. If during the darkness of this spiritual night
my gaze is fixed steadily on You, O my God, the light inun-
dating my soul at dawn will bring an abundance of happiness,
for You are leading me steadily to a closer union with You.

My soul clings fast to Thee; Thy right hand upholds me.

Like a child who needs support for its unsteady steps, O
Father, I cling to Your hand. Your Son, at Your right hand,
will protect me from all delusions of self-sufficiency and all the
snares of the enemy. May the Holy Ghost guide me to virtues
unattainable except through His gifts and fruits.

But they shall be destroyed who seek my life, they shall go into the depths of the earth.

Let all material objects, all sensory attractions, all intellectual ambitions affect my soul in vain. Of the earth, earthy, they are doomed to destruction ... through material disintegration and corruption ... through the dissipating effects of animal desires ... through the spiritual suicide resulting from human pride.

They shall be delivered over to the sword, and shall be the prey of jackals.

Through the gift of fortitude, O God, help me to use the sword of the Spirit (Eph. 6:17) against the snares and temptations of the world, the flesh, and the devil. May the holy Paraclete inspire me and sanctify me and perfect my life for eternity.

The king, however, shall rejoice in God; everyone who swears by Him shall glory, but the mouths of those who speak falsely shall be stopped.

Let me be conscious, O Lord, of the divine royalty conferred on me by Baptism. Let me reign as a true Christian, as master over all lower impulses, and rejoice in loyally keeping Your law. Let me keep my vows of fidelity to You, O eternal Truth, Who cannot be deceived by hypocrisy and perjury.

Glory be to the Father.

Glory be to the omniscience and mercy and wisdom of the most holy Trinity. May the Holy Spirit sanctify our works of mercy, dedicated to the Father of mercy, in union with His divine Son, Whose every action performed on earth revealed such tender mercy towards His creatures.

ANTIPHON: *Fear not, Mary, thou hast found grace with the Lord; behold thou shalt conceive and bring forth a Son, alleluia.*

Fear not, Mary, for you have found grace with God! Your resignation to His will is pleasing to Him; you have become the Mother of the Son of God, our Saviour and Redeemer! Pray, dear Lady, that in our own small way we may win God's favor through our devotion and fidelity . . . and thus become the happy recipients of His abundant grace . . . and effective instruments of His holy will.

ANTIPHON: *The Lord shall give unto Him.*

O blessed Lady, willing instrument in the plan of divine Providence! You furnished an abode for the King of kings and still remained the humble and pure virgin!

CANTICLE OF THE THREE CHILDREN
(Daniel 3, 57-88 and 56)

IMPERTURBABLE amidst the flaming injustice of a wicked king, Azarias, Ananias, and Misael kept their minds attentive to true values. Refusing to cringe before human power, refusing to worship false gods, they multiplied their songs of praise of You, O Lord. Far less courageous, but deeply admiring their spirit, we join in this chorus of praise, expressing our gratitude to You for preserving us amidst the temptations of the world and our own evil passions.

BLESS *the Lord, all ye works of the Lord, praise and exalt Him above all forever.*

All you works of the Lord . . . your magnitude, multitude, plenitude, your infinite variety, your perfection of detail, your regularity of recurrence . . . bless the Lord! May all you creatures be a means of raising our thoughts to the Creator!

Angels of the Lord, bless the Lord, ye heavens, bless the Lord.

All you invisible choirs, whose intellect and will have such profound capacity for praise, my Guardian Angel and all you Guardian Angels, in order to supply for the inadequacy and infrequency of human worship, help me, in this atomic age of supersonic speed, lightning calculation and superproduction, to multiply my acts of adoration. Help me to assign prayer values or attach ejaculations of praise to every inanimate object . . . to every inarticulate creature in the universe . . . and to all the indifferent actions of the day which men have not already deliberately directed to the praise of the Lord. You heavens, poised in the astronomical reaches beyond human perception . . . for every single inch of distance you are from this earth, bless the Lord!

All ye waters above the heavens, bless the Lord. All ye hosts of the Lord, bless the Lord.

All you waters that are above the heavens . . . you clouds and all the remarkable system of physical forces . . . bless the Lord. Bless the Lord, all you wonders of the colossal cosmic structure . . . whose variety and constancy and mystery . . . challenge men to spend their entire lives in pursuit of your secret operations. All you waters that are above the heavens . . . not merely waters collected in clouds, to slake the thirst of a sun-parched earth . . . but you living waters, having your source above the heavens . . . you refreshing draughts of divine grace which rain on souls scorched by the flames of passion and choked by contact with the dust of earthly desire . . . bless the Lord!

Sun and moon, bless the Lord; stars of heaven, bless the Lord.

O sun and moon, diffusing light and warmth proper to your being, be a perpetual reminder to all of us illumined by faith that we have an obligation to send or bring light and warmth to those suffering in spiritual darkness. O stars of heaven, rendering glory to God by the effect of your individual brilliance, recall to us that we, by our individual thoughts and conduct, are capable of giving Him glory . . . in spite of our remoteness from His infinite perfection. O sun and moon and stars, set in the heavens to proclaim God's love for us, remind us also to express our love for Him. O beams of light, radiating from these celestial bodies, may you represent millions of *Glorias* in praise of the most blessed Trinity! May every soul who sees the sun and moon and stars today receive the special gift of faith, or an increase of that faith, if he is already privileged to possess this priceless treasure.

Every shower and dew, bless the Lord; all ye winds, bless the Lord.

All you drops that fall to earth or form on grass or leaf or flower, may you represent countless *Glorias* in praise of the Lord. O breeze, remind me of the breath of God, and souls that must be saved for Him. O you winds, blowing in all directions, remind me of all the spirits giving constant praise to the Lord: those in Heaven, on earth, in Purgatory ... even those spirits confined to Hell, who perpetually pay homage to His punitive justice ... and those perverse spirits on earth, who try the virtue of good and noble souls, enabling them to offer sacrifice for the greater glory of God!

Fire and heat, bless the Lord; cold and chill, bless the Lord.

May all the comforts of fire and its heat remind us to bless the Lord! May every spark enkindled today, may every piece of coal and wood ... every drop of oil ... every bit of combustible material which will eventually generate heat ... represent innumerable acts of praise of the Lord, Who has so thoughtfully provided these benefits for all men! Likewise, may all men benefitted by these comforts of life receive also this day an increase of zeal for the glory of God! May all the invigorating delights of winter ... may all the tranquil pleasures of summer ... be so many occasions of raising our hearts to thank the Lord! May all the hardships endured from the cold ... may all the discomforts entailed by the heat ... be so many opportunities for sacrifice to the Lord! May the cold breeze blowing over my head ... or the uncomfortable warmth of this overheated room be a means of blessing the Lord!

Dew and rain, bless the Lord; frost and cold, bless the Lord.

May every drop of dew, refreshing the earth and early risers ... may every drop of rain, splashing down from dreary skies ... may the hoar frost, inspiring healthy souls to profit by its evanescent beauty ... signify billions and billions of ejaculations blessing the Lord! May the frost and cold, increasing the sparkle and glow of countenances ... and stimulating all with a zest for life ... bless the Lord!

Ice and snow, bless the Lord; nights and days, bless the Lord.

May every piece of ice and every flake of snow be ever

so many ejaculations expressing my love for You, O Lord! May the alternating recurrence of night and day, with all the attendant blessings of sleeping and waking hours, bless You, O Lord!

Light and darkness, bless the Lord; lightnings and clouds, bless the Lord.

May every match and candle and gas jet ... may every kilowatt of every light bulb express my love for the Light of the World. May every shadow and every cubic inch of darkness express my faith in Him Whom I cannot now perceive clearly, but only in a dark manner (1 Corinthians 13: 12). May every flash of lightning and every cloud demonstrating the power of the Lord represent so many acts of my trust in His divine care.

Let the earth bless the Lord, praise and exalt Him above all forever.

Let the earth with all its rich mineral and vegetable resources ... with all its flora and fauna ... in the abundant fertility of all its species ... bless the Lord! May it lead geologists and botanists and all other scientists to know and praise and exalt the divine Author of nature forever!

Mountains and hills, bless the Lord; everything growing from the earth, bless the Lord.

O you mountains and hills, by your very permanence in nature suggesting eternity, keep us ever mindful of eternal values! All you things that spring in the earth ... every blade of grass or shrub ... every leaf of every tree and bush ... every bud and flower ... every unit of penicillin and every other antibiotic ... bless the Creator every minute of this day!

Ye springs, bless the Lord; seas and rivers, bless the Lord.

O you drops of water in fountains, springs, seas and rivers, be for me each second of this day myriad acts of love of Him, the Source of living waters, Who said upon the Cross, "I thirst!".

Ye dolphins and all water creatures, bless the Lord; all ye birds of the air, bless the Lord.

May all you dolphins, whales and fish, submissive to divine power, as evidenced in Sacred Scripture (Cf. Tobias 11: 13; Luke 5:6) symbolize by your every movement today, acts of humility and reverence for almighty God. May all you birds, by every flap of your wings, symbolize so many acts of faith in divine Providence. May your every chirp signify many, many acts of praise of the Lord!

All ye beasts, wild and tame, bless the Lord; praise and exalt Him above all forever.

O inarticulate animals, may your every movement and sound represent acts of love and sacrifice in union with the Lamb of God, to repair for the insufficient love offered to God by men.

Ye sons of men, bless the Lord; O Israel, bless the Lord.

O sons of men, alone of all creatures endowed with speech and reason, may every breath you breathe . . . every heart beat . . . every drop of your blood . . . every movement of your body . . . every syllable spoken and heard . . . every thought expressed today . . . count as so many acts of worship, love and reverence for God, our Creator. All you privileged to have the gift of faith, bless the Lord. Multiply your prayers for others and your intentions of praise of the Lord, from your first thoughts in the morning to your last thoughts at night. May every second of your sleep and all your unconscious movements be dedicated to thanking and praising and blessing the Lord!

Priests of the Lord, bless the Lord; servants of the Lord, bless the Lord.

O priests, destined to preach divine truth, to reconcile sinners with God, and to offer up the Holy Sacrifice in adoration, reparation, thanksgiving, and supplication, may your every action and intention bless the Lord! O, all you faithful, ready to serve the Lord . . . to be submissive to His will . . . bless the Lord in all your thoughts and words and deeds!

Spirits and souls of the just, bless the Lord; holy men of humble heart, bless the Lord.

May all you whose lives are without blemish, who live according to the law of God, bless the Lord abundantly with every step you take and every inch you travel today. O holy men of humble heart, bless the Lord by countless acts of reverence for every person you see, for every sound you hear, for every cent you count, for every letter you write, for every word you read, for every image and every idea in your mind, and for every decision you make today!

Ananias, Azarias, Misael, bless the Lord; praise and exalt Him above all forever.

May all you who suffer from any cause, praise the Lord, uniting your pain and affliction with Christ in the Holy Sacrifice. May you offer each day's small crosses and trials, even petty annoyances, with the perfect oblation of Holy Mass!

Let us bless the Father and the Son and the Holy Spirit, let us praise and exalt God above all forever.

What right have we thus to usurp all the works of creation, capitalizing on their existence and monopolizing them all by a spiritual system of high finance? We may take this liberty simply because, O God, You, the Creator of all things, are our Father ... because through the merits of Your Son, we are Your adopted heirs ... and because by the inspiration of the Holy Ghost we have consecrated every moment of our lives to Your greater glory. Let us then forever, in all our thoughts, words, actions, bless You, the Father and the Son with the Holy Ghost; let us praise and magnify You in every possible way forever. In the material order, men have become immensely wealthy by dealing in scrap metal, commonly referred to as junk, or by reaping financial profit from items which others have thrown away as waste products. Similarly, can we not legitimately accumulate profit by tapping the spiritual resources provided by our environment ... by those physical, or mental, or moral fragments rejected by the world and even by some devout people, as so much junk? If we are astute merchants of the spiritual order, will we fail to ask You, O Lord, infinite in power as well as in goodness, to multiply our praises of You ... with every revolution of the wheels of the car or train in which we ride ... with every figure we write ... or key struck, as we type or play the piano ... for every hair on our head ... for every cell of our bodies ... every image ... every idea, every emotion experienced ... every judgment made or process of reasoning considered? If we spend our lives thus ... as serious traders of time for eternity ... is it likely, O divine Lord, Who said, "I must be about my Father's business" (Luke 2: 49), that You will fail to offer us the lofty spiritual values sought primarily for the glory of Your Father and for the spiritual welfare of our neighbor and ourselves?

Blessed art Thou in the firmament of heaven, praiseworthy and glorious forever!

Thus, O Lord, in spite of physical weakness ... mental lassitude . . . or moral imperfections ... we can multiply our praises of You in the firmament of heaven through all the works of Your creation. At every moment of the day ... and every second of the night ... help us to praise and glorify You with the greatest intensity forever. Learning from the lesson of the three young men in the fiery furnace ... who used their situation as a spiritual opportunity to summon even the instrument of their torture to praise You ... may we convert to heavenly profit every situation of our lives ... happily content to be scrap dealers for eternity!

ANTIPHON: *The Lord shall give unto Him the throne of David His father, and He shall reign forever.*

Through providential and prophetic preparation, O Mary, you, of all the royal line of David, were destined to become the Mother of the King of kings! Pray that, as loyal subjects of His infinite realm, we may pay worthy homage to His divine Majesty and surrender to Him willingly the complete sovereignty over our hearts.

ANTIPHON: *Behold the handmaid of the Lord.*

O Blessed Mother ... so ready and so eager to forsake your own plans to perform the will of God ... help us to be generous in His service!

PSALM 148

*P*RAISE *the Lord from the heavens, praise Him in the heights.*

O holy souls now contemplating the Beatific Vision, praise the Lord! Praise Him for us ... absorbed in the things of time. All souls in high places, pray for us sinners ... that we may learn to praise God with sincerest praise, by the imitation of Jesus Christ, His divine Son!

Praise Him, all ye His angels, praise Him, all ye His hosts.

All you celestial choirs, engaged eternally in praising the Lord ... each and every member of the nine choirs of angels ... and all you Guardian Angels ... help us to magnify the

praises of the Lord! Help us to send messages of love and praise
to Him... for every object seen... for every atom of every
created substance... for every ether wave resulting in sound
or vision, in radio and television. We know that sound or light,
diffused from a single position, results in its complete reception
in a hundred thousand television or radio sets. Spiritual values,
through the proper spiritual media, can be amplified and
multiplied to an even more astonishing degree. Hence, O pure
spirits of keenest intelligence... created to adore God forever
... will you please help to elevate our humble desires to praise
the Lord unceasingly and with great intensity? Praise Him,
all His hosts! Yes, the potential energy contained in physical
substance can be transformed into marvellous power. Yet, the
spiritual potential of created beings is much more admirable.
We call on all the hosts of heaven and earth to harness that
spiritual energy... to direct it in the form of continual praise
of God... the omnipotent Source of all energy and power.

Praise Him, sun and moon; praise Him, all ye shining stars.

O welcome luminaries, radiating joy and energy to a dark
and gloomy world, through the assistance of divine grace, may
the rays thus transmitted to each single object and person on
this earth be reflected in myriads of praise, spiraling as incense
in larger and larger circles in its ascent to the Lord!

*Praise Him, ye highest heavens, and ye waters above the
heavens.*

O you highest heavens... the state where all the saints enjoy
everlasting bliss in the presence of God... since eternity could
not be long enough to render sufficient praise to the Lord...
may each of the elect increase everlastingly in their capacity
and power for praise. Let the waters of divine grace inundate
all holy souls... that their perfection in charity may increase
their degree of everlasting glory!

*Let them praise the name of the Lord, for He commanded
and they were created.*

The universe is remarkable in its structure and operation.
Yet it cannot compare even remotely with the realm of beati-
tude, also created by God. Our Father, Who is omnipotent,
can grant us any spiritual favor. His command can obtain
for us any gift of the natural or supernatural order. May all
souls praise His name!

He established them forever and ever; He gave them a duty which shall not pass away.

God established the physical universe and the realm of the blessed forever; nor can atom bombs, or hydrogen bombs, or Russian bears destroy either. He made a law which cannot be annulled by physical or moral force, or psychological warfare. He gave to all creation a duty... and this permanent duty is to lead His children to know Him... to love Him... to glorify Him.

Praise the Lord from the earth, ye sea monsters and all depths.

Therefore, let all things of the earth... even sea monsters ... praise the Lord. The Hebrews, released from the Babylonian captivity, expressed their gratitude by calling on sea monsters and all depths of the earth to praise the Lord. The monsters of mental or physical evil are a distortion of what life should be. But these monsters of pain and depths of sorrow can be spiritually salutary: they can cause good Christians, in recoiling from them, to seek the Man of sorrows and eternal Truth. We cannot understand the problem of pain... nor even the Passion of Christ... unless we understand both in terms of love: the manifestation of God's love for man... and the opportunity for man to show his love of God. Thus, the monsters of worry and the depths of suffering can deepen one's capacity for faith and hope and love of God. Hence, we cry out with the Psalmist: "Praise the Lord, ye monsters and all depths!"

Fire and hail, snow and mist, storm winds that fulfill His word.

May all you elements of earth praise the Lord! You cannot rage without His permissive will. Then praise Him by your countless expressions of energy. Let every flicker of every flame, every piece of hail and ice, and every single flake of snow, every drop of moisture or mist, every inch passed over by every wind... praise the Lord in an unending chorus of praise!

Ye mountains and all ye hills, ye fruit trees and all ye cedars.

Mountains and hills... in virtue of the omnipresence of God sustaining you... bless the Lord! Trees bearing fruit for His living creatures, bless the Lord abundantly in all your produce! Cedars, designed by divine Providence to furnish temples for His proper worship, bless the Lord with millions of praises . . . for every inch you grow and for every foot of timber you supply for shelter!

Ye wild beasts and all tame animals, ye creeping things and ye winged fowl.

O animals, wild and tame, bless the Lord for every portion of food you supply to nourish human life! May all you other lowly creatures, whose reason for existence is not so apparent, bless the Lord in countless praises, with every single expression of the sentient life and locomotion which constitute your proper perfection!

Let the kings of the earth and all peoples, the princes and all the judges of the earth . . .

All you who hold positions of power . . . kings, princes, judges, administrators, and executives of every degree . . . let every decision you make, every direction given, every case heard, every problem solved, every item of every list consulted, every card in your files, every person interviewed, every telephone call made or received, every ceremony and every convention observed, and every detail of your duties . . . represent millions of *Glorias* in praise of the most holy Trinity today! All people subject to the commands of others, praise the Lord similarly . . . with every act executing each order . . . with every stroke of shorthand, letter typed, business entry recorded, article sold . . . for every pupil taught and every lesson imparted . . . for every nail hammered, hole drilled, every tool employed for every purpose, every piece of tile laid . . . and while travelling, for every post and tree and building passed . . . every advertisement noticed, every brick in every building, every pane of glass, every shingle on every roof . . . for every mile covered, for every red or green traffic light impeding or hastening your progress!

Young men, too, and maidens, old men and boys, praise the name of the Lord, for His name alone is exalted.

May young men and virgins, with all the purity and vigor and earnestness of youth, praise the name of the Lord for every dream and hope and ideal cherished . . . for every courtesy shown to others . . . for every bow of deference, of greeting, or farewell . . . for every effort at play or study . . . for every joy and pain experienced . . . for every attraction observed in each other! May the old with the young praise the Lord with every tick of the clock . . . for every good example or piece of advice given the young ... for every second of work or leisure ... for every recreation enjoyed, every memory rehearsed ... every step of every achievement and every failure ... for every happiness and every sorrow ... for every bit of progress made in virtue!

His majesty is above earth and Heaven, and He has lifted up the horn of His people.

The majesty of God is above heaven and earth ... incomprehensible even to the keenest intellect. Faith, a purely gratuitous gift of God, surpasses in quality the material wonders of creation, exalting us to a state where we can know to a certain degree something of the majesty of God, the secret of the earth's existence and the meaning of our own life. With faith, we perceive the solid guarantee of our hope, and we hunger to embrace the supreme Object of our faith and our hope ... in the perfect state of charity. Through divine grace, all persons ... all objects ... all activities and experiences ... can contribute to the expression of that love of God ... according to the measure of our faith, the intensity of our hope, and the amount of our charity. Let us beg daily for this divine assistance for ourselves, for our friends and relatives, for the members of our Religious Community, for our benefactors, teachers, priests, doctors, nurses, lawyers, merchants ... for our students, past, present, and future ... for our neighbors ... for the sick ... for those who will die today ... for those at the head of our government ... for leaders in all walks of life, especially for our Holy Father ... for all parents ... for those whom we shall meet today ... that all may receive an increase of the theological virtues, and that pagans at home and in foreign lands may be illumined by the gift of faith which will lead them finally to offer joyous praise to the Lord!

Be this His praise from all His faithful ones, from the children of Israel, the people close to Him.

Then let all His faithful ones, whose heroic exercise of faith and hope and love has already brought them into the very presence of God, sing hymns in His honor. Likewise, let all His faithful souls on earth, who by their thoughts, conduct, and speech, reveal that they are close followers of Christ, sing hymns of praise. May they all join in the mighty chorus of praise of the Lord, that through their merits, its quantity and quality may be increased and transformed into perfect harmony before the throne of the Most High!

Glory be to the Father.

May the existence and operation of all creation stir the minds of men to an intense and continual praise of the most holy Trinity. May this reverence and worship arising from human hearts be united to the infinite and eternal praise of the three divine Persons of the Godhead, Whose love for one another is inexhaustible and incomprehensible to creatures.

ANTIPHON: *Behold the handmaid of the Lord, be it done unto me according to Thy word.*

O Mary! Not the honor of your exalted position, but the duties it entailed, engaged your attention from the very first moment of the Annunciation of the Angel. Grant that we may be ever conscious of our serious responsibilities as chosen Spouses of Christ and privileged worshippers in His service. O humble handmaid of the Lord! Help us to cultivate your humility and ready resignation to the will of God ... that genuine praise of Him, which is not a mere tinkling cymbal.

LITTLE CHAPTER
(Isaias 11: 1-2)

*A*ND *there shall come forth a rod out of the root of Jesse, and a flower shall rise up out of his root. And the Spirit of the Lord shall rest upon Him.*

RESPONSE: *Thanks be to God.*

Isaias, favored with the gift of prophecy, foretold, thousands of years before its occurrence, Your advent, O divine Redeemer. He prophesied that You would be born of the royal line of David. Here again, as in other prophecies regarding You, O Jesus, the details are so precise and specific that there is no room for scepticism. O Holy Spirit, Who inspired the prophets to utter truth, conquer the spirit of scepticism and indifference in the world, that the spirit of faith in the one, true God may dominate the behavior of men!

HYMN

O Glorious Virgin, ever blest,
Sublime above the starry sky,
Who nurture from thy spotless breast
To thy Creator didst supply.   O Wisdom's Queen ..

What we had lost through hapless Eve
The Blossom sprung from thee restores,
And, granting bliss to souls that grieve,
Unbars the everlasting doors.   Inspiring hope ...

O Gate, through which hath passed the
*   King,*
O Hall, whence Light shone through the
*   gloom;*
The ransomed nations praise and sing
Life given from the Virgin womb.   Show us His Light ...

All honor, laud, and glory be,
O Jesu, Virgin-born, to Thee;
All glory, as is ever meet,
To Father and to Paraclete.[1]   Give Him our love.

VERSICLE: *Blessed art thou among women.*

RESPONSE: *And blessed is the fruit of thy womb.*

Our Lady, blessed among all women by the signal predilection of almighty God! By your intercessory power, obtain for us the grace to be fruitful in virtues especially pleasing to Him.

ANTIPHON: *The Holy Ghost.*

The Holy Ghost, Spirit of love and of wisdom, has come upon you, Mary, full of grace! Pray that our souls may keep always in the state of sanctifying grace and that we may realize more and more the high privilege of being temples of the Holy Ghost.

---

1 Cf. Dom Matthew Britt, O.S.B., *Hymns of the Breviary and Missal* (N. Y., Benziger, 1948), pp. 351 and 352, for this translation by R. F. Littledale.

CANTICLE OF ZACHARY
(Luke 1: 68-79)

*B*LESSED *be the Lord, the God of Israel, because He has visited and wrought redemption for His people.*

With Zachary I marvel and cry out in gratitude to You, O Lord, for Your goodness in granting the gifts of faith and redemption to Your people. I consider the number of people who lived on the same street with me ... attended the same school. I observe those I meet in public life ... on the street ... in stores ... in libraries and at professional assemblies. Relatively few of these have anything but a very confused notion of You or Your personal importance in daily life. Only about one-fifth of the total population in the United States are members of the Catholic Church. Millions throughout the world do not enjoy its benefits. I begin to be filled with awe and fear ... wondering what return, O God, You will expect from us, Your chosen ones.

And has raised up a horn of salvation for us in the house of David His servant.

You have bestowed on us the guarantees of faith. You have endowed us also with many blessings connected with this favor. You have given us Your divine Son for our Saviour, born of the royal line of David. Moreover, through the merits of our Saviour, You have raised us to the divine royalty, O God, as members of the one, true Church which offers us the means to eternal salvation.

As He promised through the mouths of His holy ones, the prophets from of old.

Down through the ages, O God, You have spoken to Your people, advising them and urging them to true worship and promising the Saviour to come. Despite those who forgot Your promises, You did not grow weary of sending Your messages of love, through Your prophets, until at last, You sent Love incarnate. Can I be indifferent to such an appeal? to such persevering consideration? to such personal concern for my salvation?

Salvation from our enemies and from the hands of all our foes.

Faith protects us from our enemies and makes us realize the impregnability of our essential, spiritual values. We are safe from the hands of all that hate us, because hate cannot enter heaven or Your Presence, O God. Even on earth, provided that we are faithful to You and live in Your Presence, we are safe from any real evil that might befall us.

He has fulfilled His kindness to our fathers and been mindful of His holy covenant.

Not out of justice merely, but from Your superabundant mercy and kindness, O God, You made a covenant with the patriarchs of old, according to which they were to obtain many blessings for keeping the faith in You, the one, true God. Sacred Scripture records many gross violations of this covenant on the part of man. The more we read the account of Your dealings with the human race and its ingratitude to You, the more we must marvel at Your divine mercy. We are grateful that You have treated man with mercy rather than with strict justice. But Zachary's utterance should provoke more personal considerations. Properly, we are shocked at the objective record of the sins of ingratitude committed by Your chosen people. But is our own record very much different, Lord? After bargaining very earnestly with You in prayer, do we not go forth and, within the matter of an hour or two, even in a minute or two, fall down before the golden calf of Self? or other lesser idols, products of ambition ... greed ... pride ... or sloth? If we were to be treated strictly according to justice, where would we be today? Are we grateful enough for Your mercy? As Sisters of Mercy, we should cultivate such gratitude to a high degree.

In the oath to Abraham our father, by which He swore to grant us ...

O God, You always kept Your part of the bargain ... in spite of our weakness ... our failings ... and our deliberate perversity. The pledge which You swore to our spiritual forefathers, You have kept, even with us who have been adopted as Your chosen followers. Let us ponder often on our rich spiritual heritage. Let us strive zealously to appreciate it by noble conduct and generous sacrifices offered to You.

That, delivered from the hands of our enemies, we should serve Him without fear.

Freedom from fear of earthly troubles is characteristic of the liberty of Your children, O God, who, delivered from the slavery of sin, serve You, their Father in heaven, as dutiful children lovingly and respectfully serve fond parents on earth. You have promised us this liberty. Have we enough confidence in You to accept it without reserve? or are we clinging to our secret idols, like the Jews of old?

In holiness and justice before Him all our days.

To serve You with great fidelity, we must be pure of heart and zealous for Your glory. Moreover, we must be just to our neighbors, whom we are to love as ourselves. This means, of course, that if we are truly grateful for Your mercy, O God, we must extend the same mercy to our neighbors, keeping in mind always the essential idea stressed in the prayer taught us by You: "And forgive us our trespasses, *as we forgive those who have trespassed against us.*" Thus, the exercise of holiness and justice will lead to the perfect state of charity ... to eternal happiness.

And Thou, O Child, shall be called the prophet of the Most High; for Thou shalt go before the Lord to prepare His ways.

The aged Zachary, by divine inspiration, knew that the vocation of His son, John the Baptist, was to prepare the world for the advent of the Messias. In a particular sense, every religious vocation has the same object ... to bring the attention of the world to Christ ... to bring the world closer to Christ. Every action as well as every prayer of ours will influence all those who observe us today. It is a *tremendous* responsibility. Are we bringing people ... our relatives and friends, our students, benefactors, casual acquaintances ... closer to Christ?

To give His people knowledge of salvation through forgiveness of their sins.

Oddly enough, one can preach Your word, O God, by keeping silent . . . especially when speech might lead to pride or to sins against charity. One can bring salvation to people through the medium of prayer and sacrifice. We admire Saint John the Baptist because of his fearless denunciation of evil conduct and his stirring exhortations to prepare Your way, O Lord, by amending bad habits. We admire him more because of his silent strength and steadiness of character . . . his renunciation and austerity. He seems actually severe in his uncompromising attitude towards sin . . . yet he preaches Your mercy, O God, through the remission of sins. Let us imitate Saint John by the intense love of You, Lord, which minimizes the value of our own ego . . . by our self-sacrifice and readiness to promote Your cause always . . . by our zeal in praying for the missions . . . by our unflinching attitude and regularity concerning the observance of Your law . . . by our attempts to extend Your kingdom and proclaim the loving kindness of Your mercy . . . by our special prayers today that particular sinners will make their peace with You.

Because of the compassionate kindness of our God with which the Orient from on high will visit us.

This condescending mercy shown us by You, O loving Father, is due to the merits of Your Son, the Light of the world, Who had chosen Saint John the Baptist "as a witness to give testimony to the light . . . that all might believe through him" (John 1: 7). Like this holy precursor, we too, must give testimony of the light and truth of our holy faith . . . by our words and particularly by our conduct . . . that, as members of the Mystical Body of Christ, we may be channels of divine mercy to all men and instruments of their salvation.

To shine on those who sit in darkness and in the shadow of death, to guide our feet into the way of peace.

Reverently rejoicing at the exalted vocation of his son, Zachary contemplated in prophetic vision the ultimate tragedy or triumph of every Christian vocation, as expressed by another Saint John: "He came unto His own and His own received Him not. But as many as received Him, to them He gave power to become the sons of God" (1: 12). Imitating both Saint Johns, willing instruments of God's mercy, we dedicate our every thought, word, deed, desire, as acts of love and zeal to bring the light to all mankind, leading them to seek the way of everlasting joy and peace.

Glory be to the Father.

Glory be to the Father, the Father of mercy, Who gave us the faith and its attendant blessings! Glory be to the Son, the Light of the world, Who helps us as members of His Mystical Body, to bring light and mercy to a world so much in need of these gifts! Glory be to the Holy Ghost, Who inspires us to dedicate our whole lives to the pursuit of divine light and the practice of Christlike mercy!

ANTIPHON: *The Holy Ghost shall come upon thee, Mary; fear not, thou shalt bear in thy womb the Son of God. Alleluia.*

The Holy Ghost has come upon you, Mary! You need not fear any material or spiritual evil. Teach us devotion to the Holy Spirit of love and peace, that we may be ever ready to imitate the example of the Prince of peace.

"Let all approach with greater confidence now than before to the throne of mercy and grace of our Queen and Mother . . ."

—Encyclical of Pope Pius XII, *Ad Coeli Reginam.*

PRIME

Hail Mary.

Hail Mary, Morning Star, Star of our hope, help us to live close to your Son today and render Him sincere and humble adoration in our every thought, word and act.

Incline unto my aid, O God. RESPONSE: *O Lord, make haste to help me.*

In these four brief hours of THE OFFICE, O Lord, we repeatedly invoke Your powerful assistance at prayer. Valiantly as we may struggle, we find it so hard sometimes to keep our attention fixed ... our voices clear ... our eyes open! Make haste to help me, Lord, that this will not be a mere mechanical repetition of lifeless words. Inject some spiritual discernment into my soul ... that I may use these prayers of praise in preparation or thanksgiving for that central act of liturgical worship, the Holy Sacrifice of the Mass ... that I may offer them together with all my acts on the paten, in union with Your divine Son, our eternal High Priest.

Glory be to the Father.

Conscious of Your divine indwelling, O Father, Son, and Holy Spirit, let me pronounce the words of the *Gloria* with profound reverence, striving to express properly their true and sacred significance.

HYMN

ℛEMEMBER, O Creator Lord,
That in the Virgin's sacred womb
Thou wast conceived, and of her flesh
Didst our mortality assume.   O Source of life ...

Mother of grace, O Mary blest,
To thee, sweet fount of love, we fly;
Shield us through life, and take us hence
To thy dear bosom when we die.   O Queen of grace ...

All honor, laud, and glory be,
O Jesu, Virgin-born, to Thee;
All glory, as is ever meet,   Help us to praise the
To Father and to Paraclete.[1]   Lord!

ANTIPHON: *O wonderful exchange!*

O admirable exchange! O remarkable opportunity for spiritual profit! The Creator stoops to earth to assume our humanity and bestows upon us a share in His divinity!

PSALM 53

O God, by Thy name save me, and by Thy might defend my cause.

O God, as I prepare to meet courageously this day's challenge, I humbly invoke the blessing of Your name and the powerful protection of Your strength.

The Hebrews, awed by Your ineffable nature, feared to address You by Your name, O God. Therefore, they referred to You by such descriptive titles as Jahweh, Elohim, Adonai ... indicative of Your supreme power and majesty. Happily, we of Christian baptism regard You under the more familiar titles of Father, Saviour, or Paraclete. In hours of severe trial, we call upon the holy name of Jesus to save us from physical and spiritual peril. We whisper the holy name into the ears of the dying ... that by it they may escape eternal damnation. Throughout all sacred prayers of the liturgy, we find the frequent recurrence of the holy name of Jesus. Indeed, there is no other name under heaven whereby our salvation is assured (Acts 4: 12). Save us then, O God, in the name of Jesus, Who

---

1 Cf. Britt, *op. cit.,* p. 352.

said, "Hitherto you have not asked anything in My name"
(John 16: 24).

And by Your might defend my cause. While the world
may look upon physical strength as the greatest guarantee of
security, true Christians pray primarily for moral and spiritual
strength, upon which they will be finally judged and defended.
But spiritual might develops from the possession of Your grace,
dear Lord, and depends on the merits of Your divine Son and
Your infinite bounty. Assist me, therefore, to rely on Your
power and strength in the realm of grace, and to strive to be
ever more closely united to You, the Source of all grace, by
Whom I shall be judged.

O God, hear my prayer; hearken to the words of my mouth.

Dear Lord, no one ever gets a busy signal when he tries to
communicate with You! Prayer is the direct line that reaches
right into Your heart. Big business boasts of its rapid communication system uniting all parts of the world. A bigger
business, centered in the world of the spirit, is the enterprise
of prayer. Hear my prayer, O Lord, for all those unconscious
of its power and value ... for those scattered and suffering in
a world of disbelief ... for those who are struggling to gain
the best from life ... for those who need You and do not know
it ... for those who wish to serve You faithfully and develop
in virtue ... for those who desire to be priests or Religious and
are having great obstacles to surmount. O God, aware of my
least concern, fear, or desire ... receive favorably all my
appeals for a world of distress and despair.

*For haughty men have risen up against me, and fierce men
seek my life; they set not God before their eyes.*

Admittedly, life is a psychological warfare, O Lord, in which
well-disguised enemy forces infiltrate our positions and sabotage
our moral strength. Ambition, pleasure, comfort, vanity, pride,
sensuality, secularism ... are some of the haughty enemies
that have risen against me ... some of the strong forces that
have sought my soul under their clever masks of duty, or principle, zeal, or sanctity, or keeping up with the times. But they
have not set You before their eyes ... nor do they aim at fulfillment of Your most holy will. Keep me spiritually strong,
dear Lord, by a ready and constant submission to the arrangements of Your providence.

Behold, God is my Helper; the Lord sustains my life.

Yes, when I am actually overwhelmed by the oppression and turmoil of surrounding events and circumstances, one glance above the horizon of human personalities and prejudices reveals You as my omnipotent helper, Who will protect my soul from succumbing to the softness characteristic of a life of ease.

Turn back the evil upon my foes; in Thy faithfulness destroy them.

Since my only real enemies are those evil forces opposed to You, destroy such demons . . . unmask their vicious characters. Assist me by Your grace to discern true and genuine eternal values and guide me in their proper attainment.

Freely will I offer Thee sacrifice; I will praise Thy name, O Lord, for its goodness.

Let me recognize, first of all, through the example of Your divine Son, the value of sacrifice as an expression of love and praise. Allow me to sacrifice to You willingly, generously, totally, that I may be recognized everywhere as a true Christian . . . as a loyal soldier, serving under the banner of Jesus Christ.

Because from all distress Thou hast rescued me, and my eyes look down upon my enemies.

Serene and secure in the impregnable realm of the supernatural life to which You have graciously raised me, I consider in a somewhat detached manner the struggle of opposing forces raging below. I breathe a devout prayer of gratitude for divine assistance. I thank You for my enemies, Lord, for they serve to purify my intentions. In fact, they have driven me to You! I ask You, dear Lord, for the grace of final perseverance in the supernatural state of Your friendship.

Glory be to the Father . . .

Glory be to the Father, Whose all-wise providence protects me, physically and spiritually, amidst all the vicissitudes of life. Glory be to the Son, Who in person has taught me the lesson of sacrifice and submission to divine Providence! Glory be to the Holy Ghost, Who guides me in the cultivation of the supernatural life! Allow me to persevere in Your service, O God, and to glorify You always! As it was in the beginning of life, is now and ever shall be, world without end. Amen.

Psalm 84

*T*HOU *hast favored, O Lord, Thy land: Thou hast restored the well-being of Jacob.*

Yes, Lord, You have blessed Your land abundantly with fruits of the field and with beauty, with sustenance for the body and the spirit. You have called us to the happiness of a superior life, by rescuing Your chosen ones from the captivity of sin . . . by bestowing on us the fruits of Your redemption . . . by endowing us with spiritual delights in the realm of beauty and truth and love which leads to eternal glory.

Thou hast forgiven the guilt of Thy people; Thou hast covered all their sins.

In spite of our repeated failures and rebellions, Lord, You have forgiven our sins . . . taken away our guilt . . . assumed the punishment due our iniquities. You have done more: You have raised us from death to an entirely new life through Your sacrifice on the Cross and its resultant graces, channeled to us through the Sacraments.

Thou has withdrawn all Thy wrath; Thou hast revoked Thy burning anger.

True, You have not removed our personal responsibility for our conduct, nor have You abrogated the law requiring temporal and eternal punishment due to sin. But You have moderated Your wrath according to the contriteness of our spirit; You have turned away from Your terrible indignation when You have seen us humble and penitent and determined to try all over again.

Restore us, O God our Saviour, and abandon Thy displeasure against us.

Restore us, O God! Change our faltering and fickle natures into noble, true and generous characters . . . that we may serve You as reliable, trustworthy friends. Turn away Your anger from us, for we are so anxious, in spite of our weakness, to be restored to Your friendship, to serve You faithfully, to love You intimately, and always to promote Your greater glory. Convert those content with mediocrity to strive zealously for perfection.

Wilt Thou be ever angry with us, prolonging Thy anger to all generations?

Dear Lord, the thought of causing You even momentary displeasure hurts us so much that we cannot imagine the horrible anguish of those who merit Your eternal condemnation. Help us, Lord, to fulfill our destiny . . . each hour and minute of it . . . according to Your providential pattern! Help us to give good example to other members of our Religious Community . . . to all Christians . . . and to all outside the faith . . . that we may not be responsible for leading succeeding generations of Your people into carelessness. Let us encourage all by our prayers and by our example to live according to Your most holy will. Grant to many of our young men and women religious vocations . . . that they may carry on Your glorious work for the benefit of succeeding generations.

Wilt Thou not instead give us life; and shall not Thy people rejoice in Thee?

O God, reconciled by the redemptive offering of Your divine Son's love, You give us sanctifying grace . . . which is new life . . . and You urge us to profit by every opportunity to win Your most precious graces. Therefore, Your people shall rejoice in You, because, although physical exercise ultimately brings weariness and exhaustion, the exercise of spiritual powers increases their facility of operation and their pleasure. Thus, the practice of charity develops the habit or virtue and, at the same time, adds to our personal happiness. Logically and psychologically, then, it must follow that we, Your people, shall rejoice in You, the more completely and the more really we become Yours in attitudes and action. The more we give to You, the happier we shall be. The more graces we seek to win for the benefit of souls and Your greater glory, the higher will be our degree of happiness in heaven.

Show us, O Lord, Thy kindness, and grant us Thy salvation.

O Lord, of all Your attributes, Your mercy and kindness are most beneficial to mankind. Grant us, then, Your tender mercy and allow us, though unworthy, to be instruments of Your mercy to others. Grant to large numbers of Your followers . . . especially to those being born this day . . . the vocation to be ministers of Your mercy, working among the poor, sick, and ignorant members of society, and influencing them to know and love You better, and to imitate the example of Your adorable Son. Give us all Your salvation, O God, which can be obtained only through Your abundant mercy, and our zeal and generosity in the practice of the corporal and spiritual works of mercy.

I will hear what God proclaims; the Lord: for He proclaims peace ...

Let me be alert, O Lord, to the promptings of Your grace. Henceforth, I shall listen to Your voice speaking within me, instead of paying attention to the worldly distractions that only disturb my soul. For You will bring peace to Your people ... the peace of a good conscience that comes from close union of thought and will with You ... the peace that comes from the recognition of truth and a firm trust in Your paternal providence.

To His people, and to His faithful ones, and to those who put in Him their hope.

To those who strive to be close to You, O Lord, You grant peace and holiness. To those who aspire to holiness, You grant Your blessing and make them saints. They must be in earnest, however: they must not merely utter noble thoughts, but they must perform heroic deeds. They must be Yours, not alone in attitude and desire, but with their whole hearts, which must know confident hope and sacrificial love. Guide us, then, Lord, both in mind and heart, and lead us along the paths of Your saints.

Near indeed is His salvation to those who fear Him, glory dwelling in our land.

You bring salvation and peace, O Lord, to those who walk the way of righteousness ... to those who fear to disobey Your commandments. Reverential fear strengthens the quality of love ... and genuine love of You leads directly to glory. Grant us, O Holy Spirit, Your gift of fear of the Lord ... that we may work out our salvation without presumption ... that we may glorify God in all our acts and finally reach the haven of eternal glory.

Kindness and truth shall meet; justice and peace shall kiss.

Mercy and truth, justice and peace, all the infinite perfections become identical in the simplicity of Your divine essence, O God! These absolutes are not just remote ideals or abstract principles. They are found in their plenitude in You ... in the three divine Persons of the Trinity. How these multiple and infinite perfections can be found in their fullness in Your simplicity, is one of the profound mysteries of Your divine nature.

Truth shall spring out of the earth, and justice shall look down from Heaven.

Truth incarnate has arisen from the earth in the person of the Word made flesh, Who said, "I am the Way, the Truth and the Life" (John 14: 6). O God, You have satisfied the claims of Your eternal justice in our behalf and You give us the means of spiritual salvation. In addition to the means for our spiritual development, O Lord, You provide well for all our temporal needs ... even though we incurred Your punishment of earning our bread by the sweat of our brow (Cf. Gen. 3: 19).

The Lord Himself will give His benefits; our land shall yield its increase.

We reflect on Your munificent goodness, O God, providing our land with food for our physical needs ... with beauty for our aesthetic enjoyment ... with truth for our intellectual satisfaction ... with faith for our spiritual comfort. According to justice, are we not under obligation to You for all these remarkable gifts? Shall we not endeavor to utilize our talents today, that they may yield good fruit? Like the faithful servant in the Gospel (Luke 19: 17, 18), should we not increase their value five-fold or ten-fold, and thus contribute to our own perfection and Your greater glory?

Justice shall walk before Him, and salvation, along the way of His steps.

Aspirations to perfection are all very laudable. Let us remember, however, dear Lord, that the very foundation for this superstructure of holiness is to be found in the observance of the cardinal virtues, particularly that of justice. Seeking exalted gifts of grace will not be favored by You, if we do not observe Your law with regard to our neighbors, and cultivate the natural virtues. You would have us be courteous and civil to our fellowmen ... members of the Mystical Body of Christ. Justice shall walk before You ... Salvation shall walk along the way of Your steps. Help us, therefore, O Lord, today to follow in the path of justice ... to observe its principles ... to assume its human responsibilities ... and thus to walk most surely the way of our salvation. (Cf. Psalm 118.)

Glory be to the Father.

Glory be to the Father, Source of eternal truth and justice
... and to the Son, the Word, Who taught us on earth the
principles of eternal truth and justice ... and to the Holy Spirit,
Who guides the Church unfailingly in matters of eternal truth
and justice! As it was in the beginning, is now, and ever shall
be, world without end. Amen. May we learn progressively
to recognize Your truth, to seek Your justice, to enjoy Your
mercy, and attain Your everlasting peace!

Psalm 116

Praise the Lord, all ye nations; glorify Him, all ye peoples!

Render praise for all His benefits, O all people of all nations!
Were you privileged to sit as your country's representative
at the United Nations' deliberative assemblies, you would feel
that a great responsibility was yours. You now enjoy a more
exalted privilege, involving a greater responsibility. This new
day has been given you to praise the Lord in the name of your
respective nation, for all His gifts of the material and spiritual
order ... not the least of which are His love and peace. Praise
the Lord, therefore, in your every act ... in your every word
... in your every thought! Join in the mighty chorus of
adoration and thanksgiving which the Church directs in her
liturgy today!

*For steadfast is His kindness toward us, and the fidelity of
the Lord endures forever.*

We have a greater responsibility to render praise to God,
since we are conscious through deep faith of the infinite mercy
He has shown us. Our obligation of gratitude remains to Him
forever, because of His steadfast fidelity ... His justice ... His
kindness ... and His peace.

Glory be to the Father.

May we spend each moment of the day, therefore, at times
of work, or recreation, or formal prayer, in making acts of
love and gratitude to the Father, and to the Son, and to the
Holy Ghost! May we spend each new day in a similar manner, as a preparation for our office of praise for all eternity!

ANTIPHON: *O wonderful exchange! The Creator of mankind, taking a body with a living soul, vouchsafed to be born of a Virgin; and becoming man without man's concurrence, made us partakers of His divine nature.*

O admirable exchange! The Creator of mankind, assuming our flesh, consented to be born of a virgin; and proceeding as man without man's concurrence, has bestowed upon us His Godhead! As we pray in the Offertory of the Mass, O Lord, grant that we may share in an ever-increasing degree Your Godhead, since You have deigned to share our manhood!

LITTLE CHAPTER
(Canticle of Canticles 6: 9)

*W*HO *is she that comes forth as the morning rising, fair as the moon, bright as the sun, terrible as an army set in array?*

Unparalleled beauty provokes wonder in the minds of the beholders. Physical beauty combined with power is admirable. Here, the superhuman beauty and strength are applied to you. Our Lady, since you come forth with all the supernatural splendor of your immaculate virginal purity, *beautiful as the dawn!* As Queen of heaven, you are more lovely than the moon or any other celestial body! As Seat of Wisdom, you are more *brilliant than the sun* and, as Mother of divine grace, you are the fairest of creatures, reflecting the rays of divine light and love to man. Yet, you are *terrible as an army in battle array*, because of your supremacy against all evil adversaries and your great intercessory power before the throne of God. O Mary, teach me to appreciate the fact that every soul in the state of grace also comes forth each day as the morning rising, fair as the moon, bright as the sun, terrible as an army set in order of battle. Teach me to respect others because of the possible or real supernatural beauty of their souls ... to pray that this beauty may be enhanced by an increase of grace ... and may be preserved forever for their own happiness and the eternal glory of God!

RESPONSE: *Thanks be to God!*

Thanks be to God ... that we have such a model ... that we have such an advocate ... that we have such a representative of the human race before the heavenly throne!

TERCE

$\mathcal{W}$HEN *Thou wast born . . .*

When You were born, O divine Infant, O Messiah! Then were the prophecies of patriarchs and prophets fulfilled. O Hope of all nations, fulfill as certainly our desires and hopes for eternal life!

PSALM 119

$\mathcal{I}$N *my distress I called to the Lord, and He answered me.*

Whenever I have suffered trials or troubles . . . whenever I have felt discouraged, disappointed, sick, or weary . . . whenever I have encountered difficulties in accomplishing something, or felt limited in my power to help others in distress . . . I have cried to You, O Lord, and You have heard me.

O Lord, deliver me from lying lip, from treacherous tongue.

But *this* trial is so much harder to bear than the others, Lord! It calls to my sensitive nature for retaliation! Everything about it makes me want to settle the issue by doubling up my fists and deliver telling blows to the individuals causing this disorder! I know that I have many faults, Lord, but why must they tell lies about me? malign me? say things that are grossly unfair and unjust? attribute unworthy motives to me? misinterpret my every action and even my thoughts? How can I act in a supernatural manner in the face of all that? Lord, deliver my soul from lying lips, and from treacherous tongues.

What will He inflict on thee, with more besides, O treacherous tongue?

With the Apostles, O Lord, I am anxious to defend myself with the sword ... or at least to ask You to settle these vicious slanderers definitely and finally with atomic fire and brimstone.

Sharp arrows of a warrior with fiery coals of brushwood.

Yet, it brings small consolation to me to know that these calumniators may have as their reward everlasting companionship with the father of lies; nor does it relieve me to know that the evil darts inflicted on others will eventually revert towards themselves ... bringing them misery and desolation. When those maligners are causing me great mental torture, it does not make me more serene to reflect that they are preparing to enter an abode of eternal hate.

Woe is me that I sojourn in Mosoch, that I dwell amid the tents of Cedar!

Dear Lord! I am so distressed at all these unkind criticisms ... these unjust suspicions ... when I have been trying so hard to do my best in Your service! I am surprised and even a little hurt, I must admit, to think that even You would allow such things! They are almost intolerable! If I could only retaliate and gain some degree of vengeance! Why should civilized people act so much like barbarians!

All too long have I dwelt with those who hate peace.

I feel so hostile towards everyone. ... Even those I thought I could depend on, seem so ready to believe untruths about me! How can I be serene and calm and tranquil among those who hate peace?

When I speak of peace, they are ready for war.

Suddenly my soul is flooded with supernatural light: I understand at last, my God! Your peace is won at a great price. It involves many battles and much bloodshed. Amidst all this bitter resentment and self-pity and childish desire for revenge, there arises the majestic figure of Christ among His enemies. There stands our Lord, Who came on earth to save all men ... Who gave His life for all men ... rejected, maligned, crucified by men ... deserted even by His disciples! I have my choice: I can defend myself against the assaults of all who oppose me ... or I can look upon the face of Christ, remaining

calm and peaceful even among those who jeered at Him and
mocked Him ... among those who tried to trap Him in His
speech, so that they could testify against Him. Is this the
opportunity You are giving me to seek Your peace, O Lord?
to imitate You, even in a very small way? Am I courageous
enough to enter the conflict against myself ... to face valiantly
the shedding of blood ... to win Your peace? O Queen of peace,
teach me nobility of spirit!

Glory be to the Father.

Glory be to the Father, Who protects me against all enemies!
Glory be to the Son, Who redeemed me and taught me how
to use my enemies as a spiritual endowment! Glory be to the
Holy Ghost, Who sanctifies me and guides me in the supernatural warfare against my enemies! As it was in the beginning, is now and ever shall be, world without end. Amen.
May God be good enough to help me forgive my enemies ...
to pray daily for them ... and always to regard adverse criti-
cism as a means of keeping my intention pure.

PSALM 120

*I lift up my eyes toward the mountains; whence shall help
come to me?*

Confidently, I raise my eyes to You, O Maker of the mountains, whenever I need help in the struggles of life. Daily I
pray for an increase of faith ... for the faith that will remove
mountains, if necessary. I pray for the spread of Your kingdom
on earth ... that it may rise above the mountainous barriers
of hostility and prejudice as certainly as it has penetrated all
parts of the globe. O omnipotent Father, improve the quality
of my service and increase the quantity of believers!

My help is from the Lord, Who made Heaven and earth.

There is no doubt, O Lord, that You will respond to my least
glance of alarm or appeal. Before I can formulate an earnest
plea, You are aware of my plight, You have foreseen it and
You are close at hand to assist me. For You, the Creator of
heaven and earth, are omniscient as well as omnipotent. You
are deeply concerned for my welfare. More swiftly than television, radio, or radar, You respond to the distress signal of
my spirit.

May He not suffer thy foot to slip; may He slumber not Who guards thee.

As we pray to the Lord for assistance, the Holy Spirit re-assures us: "He will not suffer your foot to be moved, nor will He slumber that keepeth you." Therefore, let us not fret about the future, since our Lord Himself while on earth described His providential care of His creatures. Divine Providence observes all details of our existence better than we would be able to imagine. Like a fond mother, hovering over her sick child, the Lord regards all our behavior and He watches every thought, impulse, and desire of our hearts and minds. Nor does He grow weary, or sleepy, or bored ... nor does He employ a substitute, since this interest issues from His infinite love.

Indeed He neither slumbers nor sleeps, the guardian of Israel.

Within our hearts, O Lord, we know that You will never fail to assist Your chosen followers. Infinitely beyond human limitations and human weaknesses, You can always be trusted, although all other guarantees of security and safety collapse. When political and social conditions alarm us ... when mortal disasters or disease threaten ... when mental or moral crises jeopardize our salvation ... there is no need for men of staunch faith to fear, since, O Lord, You will care for Your people. When You delay an immediate response to our prayers, it is simply to test our faith and hope ... to increase our capacity for love.

The Lord is thy guardian; the Lord is thy shade; He is beside thee at thy right hand.

The Holy Spirit helps us recall illustrations of Your concern for us. Long before we ever existed, O Lord, You planned the details of our lives. Later, You placed us among devoted parents, relatives and friends ... You conferred upon us the special graces of Your sacraments. You provided a fitting education and the privilege of a high vocation. You are concerned with our welfare every single moment of our existence ... in every action of our lives!

The sun shall not harm thee by day, nor the moon by night.

Evidence of Your concern for us can be observed in the system and control of cosmic forces. Solar and lunar energies, tremendous as they are, work for our benefit, not for our harm. Confidence, then, should be the keynote of our attitude towards all new scientific discoveries. O Lord, You will not allow the elements of Your creation to annihilate man, the most favored of Your creatures. If man, however, uses his intellect and will for the perverse and sinister purpose of destroying himself and his fellow men, You will still protect Your people ... those who have faith and confidence in You ... because no atomic energy can reach the recesses of the spirit, nor can psychological warfare wound a soul which remains firmly united with You.

The Lord will guard thee from all evil; He will guard thy life.

The prayer we utter, for our own souls and for the soul of each member of the Mystical Body of Christ, is this: May the Lord keep us from any moral evil! May He keep our souls always in the state of sanctifying grace! May He keep us more and more closely united to Him, so that no genuine harm can befall us!

The Lord will guard thy coming and thy going, both now and forever.

Our prayer continues: May the Lord protect us in all our contacts with the outside world! May He help us to influence other souls whom we meet and lead them to increased fervor in His service! May He deepen our capacity for love and prayer! May he strengthen the bond of our friendship with Him and our power to glorify Him for all eternity!

Glory be to the Father.

Glory be to the Father, Whose providential concern protects us! Glory be to the Son, Whose merits provide for our spiritual security! Glory be to the Holy Ghost, Whose loving guidance urges us along the certain way of everlasting salvation! As it was in the beginning, when we had only potential existence in the divine mind ... is now, when we enjoy all the benefits of real existence ... and ever shall be, when we shall have realized the highest purpose of our existence according to God's plan ... may the Lord be forever adored and glorified!

Psalm 121

I rejoiced because they said to me, "We will go up to the house of the Lord."

Devout Hebrews rejoiced over their privilege of worshipping You in the beautiful temple of Jerusalem, O God! Even those who lived at a considerable distance made every effort to visit the temple at least once a year, or on solemn feasts. This was the ancient center of public worship, where all the tribes of Judah journeyed to offer praise to You. Here Your law was promulgated and dispensed. Here ritualistic ceremonies were performed in Your honor. Here the high priests offered sacrifice and led Your people in prayer.

Faithful Catholics have far greater reasons to rejoice. We can enter into Your very presence in the Blessed Sacrament without going on a long pilgrimage. We are closely united to You, O Jesus, our eternal High Priest, as we kneel to express our private prayers, or follow the public liturgical worship. As Religious, we enjoy a more exalted state of happiness. We are privileged to dwell under the same roof with You. We form, as it were, the intimate circle of Your immediate family. Hence, the soul called to the Religious life rejoices exceedingly to hear the whispering of Your divine Wisdom: "We shall go up to the house of the Lord."

And now we have set foot within thy gates, O Jerusalem . . .

Yes, looking back at the magnificence and glory that was once yours, O Jerusalem, city of God, prototype of Christ's Church, and symbol of the Kingdom of heaven, we realize that, according to God's plan, we were already standing in your courts. May our humble and generous correspondence with the designs of a merciful providence prevent in us the sins that would merit our utter destruction and our Lord's severe condemnation! (Cf. Matt. 24: 2.)

Jerusalem built as a city with compact unity.

Jerusalem, built as an impregnable city, O my God, was strong in its external fortifications. Its inherent strength, however, depended on the inner spiritual energy and union of its inhabitants. When these forces declined, the city succumbed to external assault. Similarly, it seems, the spiritual strength of the followers of Christ depends on the quality and degree of charity practiced by the members of His Mystical Body.

We Religious ... through prayer, teaching, and good example ... are in a strategic position to promote this inner spiritual union and strength of Your household, O Lord!

To it the tribes go up, the tribes of the Lord, according to the decree for Israel, to give thanks to the name of the Lord.

All Jews of high or low estate gathered in the temple of Jerusalem to worship You, dear Lord! In our churches, the faithful of all classes unite in public prayer and offer the Holy Sacrifice of the Mass. Many rejoice in the added privilege and responsibility of uniting several times a day for the purpose of praising You. All participants in liturgical worship ... such as those sharing in the Sacrifice of the Mass and those reciting the sacred Hours of THE OFFICE ... render formal testimony of praise. Exultantly, the members of the Mystical Body of Christ can swell their praises to infinite measure, through union with their divine Head and High Priest!

In it are set up judgment seats, seats for the House of David.

Formidable was the power of the ancient judges, authorities on Your law ... for the sincerity of worship has always been considered contingent on moral conduct. We who have been redeemed by You, O Jesus, revere profoundly Your divine power as supreme judge, but we also adore You with gratitude, because You have provided the graces which will guide us to moral integrity ... the essential basis for sanctity.

Pray for the peace of Jerusalem! May those who love Thee prosper!

One grace You grant, for example, is the inspiration to pray for all other members of Your kingdom. Therefore, we earnestly pray for all those inhabitants of Your kingdom on earth ... that they may enjoy Your peace ... that they may enjoy the abundance of Your graces ... that they may enjoy the delights of Your personal love.

May peace be within thy walls, prosperity in thy buildings.

Let us say with You, O divine Master, Who taught us how to pray: "Thy kingdom come!" We ask that peace and charity forever unite the members of the faithful ... we pray that all within the Church may receive manifold spiritual and temporal blessings.

Because of my relatives and friends I will say, "Peace be within thee!"

Particularly do we specify in our intentions the needs of our relatives and friends. Above all other considerations, we desire for each of them the interior peace which the world cannot give . . . the peace that comes from faith in You, O God, from resignation to Your holy will, and from the contentment of a good conscience.

Because of the house of the Lord, our God, I will pray for thy good.

Nevertheless, our obligation does not stop with our immediate relatives and friends. We pray for our neighbors from other lands . . . for Cardinals Wyszynski, Mindszenty, and Stepinac, and for Archbishop Beran . . . for all the priests and nuns and other good people who are suffering in foreign fields for the cause of religion. We must pray for all the needs of the Church . . . for the missions at home and abroad . . . for vocations . . . for all the intentions of our Holy Father . . . for bishops, superiors, and all those burdened by economic, domestic, social and spiritual problems. We are so grateful to God that we possess the gift of prayer!

Glory be to the Father.

Glory be to the Father, Who long ages ago arranged for our residence in the house of the Lord! Glory be to the Son, Who ever dwells near us in His tabernacle in the house of the Lord! Glory be to the Holy Ghost, Who guides us by His inspirations concerning the proper spirit of service in the house of the Lord! May we profit spiritually for ourselves and all mankind by our dwelling in the house of the Lord . . . may we persevere in His loving, joyous, and everlasting service!

ANTIPHON: *When Thou wast born of a Virgin, after an ineffable manner, the Scriptures were then fulfilled. Thou didst descend like rain upon the fleece, that Thou mightest save mankind. We praise Thee, O our God.*

When You were born, O divine Saviour, in a most marvelous manner, of a Virgin, then were the Scriptures fulfilled. When You engendered our spirits in the virginal purity of Your redeeming sacrament of Baptism . . . then was Your promise of redemption fulfilled in an ineffable manner. As rain descending upon the sheep washes and quietly cleanses their fleece from all sordid contact with earth, so Your abundant grace has

come down upon the human race to transform it into supernatural loveliness. We praise You, O God, Who, through Your
supreme love, has made such a transformation possible!

LITTLE CHAPTER
(Ecclesiasticus 24: 15)

*And so was I established in Sion, and in the holy city like-
wise I rested, and my power was in Jerusalem.*

O Mary! The Wisdom of divine Providence, directing the
course of events from the beginning of the world, has chosen
you as the Mother of our incarnate Lord. Lead us in the ways
of heavenly wisdom through the imitation of the virtues of
His earthly life.

VI

SEXT

*I*N *the bush which Moses saw.*

As the bush which Moses saw, most holy Mother, was a symbol of your virginity, pray that the ardor of our love and the purity of our lives may consume all the dross of the holocaust we wish to offer to God!

PSALM 122

*T*o *Thee I lift up my eyes Who art enthroned in Heaven.*

When physical or moral ills assail me, I feel all the burden and weakness of my human nature. Contrition for all the sins of my life . . . remorse for all my mistakes . . . grief at my very mediocrity . . . bow my head in guilty sorrow. Discouraged but not despairing, I lift my eyes prayerfully and hopefully to You, O Lord, dwelling in the heavens.

Behold, as the eyes of servants are on the hands of their masters, As the eyes of a maid are on the hands of her mistress, So are our eyes on the Lord, our God, till He have pity on us.

We admit our sins merit Your punishment, O Lord, and for that reason we are almost afraid to raise our eyes to You in our sorrow. We sinners have lost Your friendship, O God, and deserve not to look upon Your sacred countenance. The Hebrews, often suffering the humiliation of captivity, knew what it meant to be in servitude. They knew that the slave scarcely ventures to gaze upon the face of his master or mistress, but often raises his eyes only as far as their hands . . . fearful lest these powerful instruments may at any time wield his punishment. Like slaves, then, O Lord, we fear You and Your just punishments, until You will have mercy on us and once again restore us to the intimacy of Your friendship.

Have pity on us, O Lord, have pity on us, for we are more than sated with contempt.

By Your infinite mercy, O Lord, blot out all our sins and offences, protect us from the errors of our own stupidity, and preserve us from a lukewarm and laggardly performance in Your service. We feel so vile and mean, Lord, not only at the thought of offending You, Who are all good, but we despise ourselves for ever offering You anything less than our best efforts.

Our souls are more than sated with the mockery of the arrogant, with the contempt of the proud.

Truly we are miserable: A sensitive conscience overwhelms us with grief for our sins. Those who are rich in this world's goods despise us, Lord, and those who are haughty and proud gaze at us with disdain. Material prosperity or mental superiority would not alleviate our condition. Moral power alone will deliver us from destruction. Help us, O Lord, to be truly humble and contrite ... that we may win Your grace to be morally strong, no matter what our economic, or social, or intellectual status may be.

Glory be to the Father.

Glory be to the Father, Who allows us to suffer for our sins! Glory be to the Son, Who teaches us the value of suffering! Glory be to the Holy Ghost, Who helps us to profit by suffering! Daily may we share our sufferings with the Man of sorrows, that they may be raised through His infinite merits to an eternal oblation agreeable in Your sight, O heavenly Father!

PSALM 123

Had not the Lord been with us, let Israel say ...

When we consider the dangers we have passed through, and all the hazards of modern living ... when we hear accounts of all the accidents and ills that have befallen others ... we begin to feel a great deal of gratitude to You, O Lord, for Your protection of us and of our families and friends.

Had not the Lord been with us: when men rose up against us, then would they have swallowed us alive.

Of course, Lord, cannibals are rather uncommon, but the Psalmist here suggests that moral evils are much more to be dreaded than physical harm. If our enemies in the spiritual struggle viciously attack us through the lips of men, certainly the effects can be more devastating than any physical encounter, even with a cannibal. If You are with us, however . . . if we have the grace to retain our peace of soul and our trust in You amidst all malicious attacks . . . then we will be spiritually secure, no matter how overpowering may be the threat of our opponents.

When their fury was inflamed against us, then would the waters have overwhelmed us.

Although the enemies of goodness may rage and storm, O omnipotent Lord, You will always preserve us from harm, if we simply do our best and rely on Your infinite mercy.

The torrent would have swept over us; over us then would have swept the raging waters.

Uncontrolled forces of nature can cause tremendous damage to life and property. Unrestrained human powers can cause irreparable moral ruin. Our souls, dwelling amidst these physical forces and human powers, would certainly have been overwhelmed with their superior might, O Lord, were it not for Your ever-vigilant favor . . . for You know our weakness so much better than we can realize it.

Blessed be the Lord, Who did not leave us a prey to their teeth.

Daily do we bless You, O Lord, because You have preserved us from the forces of evil, and even from our own natural dispositions and tendencies that would make us the prey of malevolent spirits. One example of the way You have preserved us from being "a prey to their teeth" is in the Religious vocation which You have granted to us. Here, under the discipline of the vows and our holy Rule, we are protected from many of the associations and temptations of those not favored by living in such a blessed state.

We were rescued like a bird from the fowlers' snare.

By Your grace, O God, we elude the diabolical snares and traps calculated to endanger our purity of soul. Again and again, O God, You have granted us a favorable reply to the last petition of the *Our Father.* "Deliver us from evil," for we are so often as little birds, caught in a net of circumstances from which we could never happily extricate ourselves without Your divine aid.

Broken was the snare, and we were freed.

Even when we are caught temporarily in the meshes of evil through our own fatal blundering, dear Lord, You are ready to save us through the Sacrament of Penance. Thus, we are released from the broken snare . . . to soar once more in the free atmosphere of faith. Liberated there, we can outsing the soaring sparrow . . . making our praise resound unto the very courts of Heaven. We can outsoar the singing sparrow, winging our way into Your majestic Presence!

Our help is in the name of the Lord, Who made Heaven and earth.

We need not fear the vindictiveness of opposing powers, for our help is in Your name, O Lord . . . in the omnipotent power of Jesus . . . Saviour of the world . . . in the creative power of the Father, Who made heaven and earth . . . in the omniscient wisdom of the Holy Spirit, Who resides in our soul as in a temple, making it spiritually secure while it is in the state of sanctifying grace.

Glory be to the Father.

Glory be to the Father, Who created us and constantly sustains us! Glory be to the Son, Who redeemed us and is still willing to save us! Glory be to the Holy Ghost, Who guides us and helps us elude the snares of the enemy! May our souls remain always in the state of sanctifying grace, that we may forever glorify You and be eternally safe with You in Heaven!

PSALM 124

THEY who trust in the Lord are like Mount Sion, which is immovable; which forever stands.

The splendor and beauty and magnificence of Mount Sion are but symbols of the spiritual light and beauty that flood the soul endowed with the theological virtues. The mighty temple of Jerusalem was one day to be destroyed, but the soul possessing the gift of faith need never yield to external assault. It can be destroyed only by its refusal to believe and hope in You, Lord, and to love You as our heavenly Father.

Mountains are round about Jerusalem; so the Lord is round about His people, both now and forever.

Your commandments ... Your precepts ... Your counsels ... the particular rule of life laid down for Your followers ... are so many steep mountains by which You keep us safe. The mountains, solid symbols of eternity, suggest the permanence and stability of law and justice based on eternal truth. More reliable than any symbols, however, is Your Eucharistic Presence amidst Your people and Your frequent personal visits to the heart of every believer.

For the scepter of the wicked shall not remain upon the territory of the just, Lest the just put forth to wickedness their hands.

Although evil forces sometimes appear to have supremacy in the political, social, and economic world, O Lord, You will not allow them to triumph to the detriment of Your true followers. You do not permit the just and righteous to be tempted beyond their strength. You always assist with divine grace those who are loyal and true to You, because You are anxious that they remain Your faithful friends.

Do good, O Lord, to the good, and to the upright of heart.

Be kind, O Lord, to those who are striving valiantly to do what they believe to be right ... to those who are trying to correspond to Your will made manifest in the daily circumstances of life ... to those who worship You truly in their hearts, although they may be timid at times of formal prayer and, like the publican, just kneel at a distance (Cf. Luke 18: 13), humbly acknowledging their misery and begging Your mercy.

But such as turn aside to crooked ways, may the Lord lead away with the evildoers! Peace be upon Israel.

Of course, You are just, O Lord! You will reward the good ... but You will punish the wicked. Moreover, to insure the peace and tranquility of Your eternal city, You must punish also those self-righteous souls who have stooped to perverse ways ... either because their zeal was thwarted or their pride piqued. They have placed their own will above Yours. If stubbornly defiant, they will scarcely be fitting inhabitants of Your realm of peace, for which they have been destined.

Glory be to the Father.

Glory be to the Father, Whose laws protect us! Glory be to the Son, Whose Presence sustains us! Glory be to the Holy Ghost, Whose truth inspires us! Help us, O God, to keep faithfully Your commandments, receive reverently Your personal visits, execute courageously Your noble inspirations ... that we may dwell forever in the joyous and peaceful contemplation of the Beatific Vision!

ANTIPHON: *In the bush which Moses saw burning without being consumed, we acknowledge thine admirable virginity preserved. Intercede for us, O Mother of God,.*

O Mother of God, intercede for us, your children, who wish to offer up a pure sacrifice ... a complete sacrifice ... a perfect sacrifice ... in union with our High Priest, your Son!

LITTLE CHAPTER
(Ecclesiasticus 24: 16)

*A*ND *I took root in an honorable people, and in the portion of my God His inheritance; and my abode is in the full assembly of saints.*

The holy season of the Nativity causes us to esteem more and more the wisdom of God and the great gifts He prepares for His children. May we imitate you, O Mary, so willing to receive the Holy Spirit. Thus, shall we struggle to remain permanently among the *honorable* souls in the state of grace ... and consider the spiritual possessions the only desirable inheritance ... that we may dwell forever among the assembly of saints.

VII

NONE

*B*EHOLD, *Mary*.

Behold, Mary has brought forth divine fruit by her simple
fiat! May she teach us, as we contemplate the mystery of the
Incarnation, the peace and happiness that comes with complete
submission to the divine will.

PSALM 125

*W*HEN *the Lord brought back the captives of Sion, we were
like men dreaming.*

O Lord, when You released the Jews from their state of servitude in Babylon, their joy was unbounded. In modern times,
the longed-for escape from the tortures of concentration camps
brings relief beyond the power of description.

*Then our mouth was filled with laughter, and our tongue
with rejoicing.*

When You deliver us from physical or mental anguish, our
happiness of spirit must overflow into words and actions: we
desire to communicate our joy to our neighbors ... we want to
express our gratitude to You.

*Then they said among the nations, "The Lord has done
great things for them."*

We can easily understand that the Hebrews, delivered from
captivity, would desire to demonstrate their exuberant joy to
all nations. They sang as a sign of their joy, so that all people
knew that You had done great things for them. Do people
recognize from our behavior, Lord, that we have been favored
by Your divine Majesty?

The Lord has done great things for us; we are glad indeed.

The deliverance of the Hebrews from bondage seems quite remote, although we can appreciate the happiness brought by the release of modern prisoners. We know, too, the intense emotion of joy and gratitude welling up in our hearts at the thought of what Your adorable Majesty has done personally for each one of us. You have released us through Baptism from the captivity of original sin... a captivity endured for thousands of years by our ancestors... You have released us through the Sacrament of Penance from the captivity deserved by our own sins. Through the grace of a religious vocation, You have released us from the captivity of the world and its enchanting allurements. Finally, through the portals of death, You will release us from all bonds of earth, that our spirits will be perfectly free to adore You in peace forever.

Restore our fortunes, O Lord, like the torrents in the southern desert.

Turn this captivity of earth to our permanent spiritual profit, O Lord! Through a peculiar paradox symbolized by Your Cross, turn our hardships into gifts for Your glory. With the power and velocity and relief of a southern torrent, turn our temporal misery into eternal joy!

Those that sow in tears shall reap rejoicing.

Tears alone, we realize, do not merit any reward. Those who valiantly sow the seeds of spiritual virtues... those who water those seeds abundantly with tears of consecrated sorrow, but not of bitterness... will one day, with Your blessing, O God, reap the rich harvest of their arduous endeavors.

Although they go forth weeping, carrying the seed to be sown . . .

Throughout Sacred Scripture the spiritual life is compared to the work of a planter. The wise man is the one who procures a good yield for his labor. Grant, O Lord, that as Your hired laborers we may engage seriously and soberly and steadily in this business of planting... so that in fields made fertile by Your grace, we may joyously reap the reward of our feeble efforts magnified by Your infinite mercy. Let our weeping be not that of immature or cynical grumblers, but let it be a symbol of our union with Christ, Who wept (Cf. Luke 19: 41) at the prospect of so many souls rejecting His grace and their own salvation.

They shall come back rejoicing, carrying their sheaves.

Like the planters of all ages, we contemplate with admiration and with joy the marvelous wonders of Your creation, O God, since by Your grace You vivify even in hostile soil the seeds scattered by our labors and sufferings. You allow them to germinate and blossom and fructify into the abundant reaches of Christian virtue.

Glory be to the Father.

Glory be to the Father, Who cursed the earth, yet allows it to yield by the sweat of man's brow! Glory be to the Son, Who redeemed us from the captivity of the earth! Glory be to the Holy Ghost, Who inspires us to sow wisely in virtues that we may reap well our salvation! May the Lord bless abundantly our labors for Him during life and our love for Him through eternity!

Psalm 126

*U*NLESS *the Lord builds the house, they labor in vain who build it.*

O master Architect of the universe! You know the secrets of safe construction. Those who ignore Your advice in building their spiritual edifice are risking certain disaster. The Tower of Babel is a symbol which bears witness to unwise human planning.

Unless the Lord guard the city, in vain does the guard keep vigil.

Human prudence is futile unless it relies on divine wisdom. The United Nations' efforts for peace are doomed to fail, while the members exclude You from their parleys, O divine Prince of peace!

It is vain for you to rise early, or to put off your rest ...

Naturally and supernaturally we need the light of heaven to achieve success in our labors. Our nature requires that we relax, rest tranquilly, and wait for the light before rising to "earn our bread by the sweat of our brow" (Gen. 3: 19). Our spiritual stability, too, O adorable Majesty, requires dependence on the light of divine grace.

You that eat hard-earned bread, for He gives to His beloved in sleep.

Sleep is a wonderful gift, O my God! We enjoy it and thank You for it. Ambition and industry not blessed by You will result in useless striving. You have shown us, O Lord, that if peace and patience of soul prepare the way for our prayer ... then Your truth will illumine our minds, through the rites of liturgical worship.

Behold, sons are a gift from the Lord; the fruit of the womb is a reward.

You allow men to be Your instruments, bringing Your gifts to others ... yet our own feeble efforts could never produce these gifts without You, O divine Giver! We witness the gift of life, bestowed by Your personal creation of each human soul. Children are Your precious gifts, Lord ... the reward of marital union. A direct blessing of Yours, they cause us to marvel at the mystery of life. Your spiritual blessings far surpass the quality and quantity of human labor. Gratefully, we rejoice that our intermittent striving can never limit the graces bestowed by Your infinite goodness and love.

Like arrows in the hand of a warrior are the sons of one's youth.

Israel may have been subjected to nations having greater military power; but she was spiritually strong in her numerous descendants who kept alive her deep faith in You, the one, true God. Similarly, in the social and political world of today ... might and glamor and superficial polish often dazzle and impress the ignorant, but those favored souls who practice ardent faith in You will receive manifold spiritual blessings.

Happy the man whose quiver is filled with them; they shall not be put to shame when they contend with enemies at the gate.

Blessed is the man who has cooperated with You, O Lord, according to the capacities of his nature. You will elevate and transform his nature by gifts of the natural and supernatural order. When Your faithful servant will meet his enemies, ready to attack the citadel of his soul, he can confidently rely on You, residing within his soul. When these enemies threaten the very destiny of the faithful adorer, You will receive Your servant within the gates of Your everlasting dwelling.

Glory be to the Father.

Glory be to the Father, Who has endowed us with supernatural life! Glory be to the Son, Whose supreme love has
taught us the value of this life! Glory be to the Holy Ghost,
Who illumines our hearts and minds to appreciate and strive
for the eternal preservation of this life!

PSALM 127

ℋ𝒶𝓅𝓅𝓎 *art thou who fearest the Lord, who walkest in His
ways!*

All who truly revere You and serve You devoutly, O infinite
Majesty, will receive Your abundant blessings ... for resignation to Your most adorable will is the secret of all sanctity.

*For thou shalt eat the fruit of thy handiwork; happy shalt
thou be, and favored.*

Although You depend not on our labor or our devotion for
the manifold favors You bestow, You have allowed us to share
in Your benefits through the physical and volitional energies
we exert to show our love for You or Your human creatures.
If we have Your love and blessing, nothing else really matters
... where, or how, or by whom we are employed ... since we
are acquiring a spiritual treasury of merits in Your honor for
the salvation of ourselves and our fellow men.

*Thy wife shall be like a fruitful vine in the recesses of thy
home; Thy children like olive plants around thy table.*

O God, You have promised fecundity to the early patriarchs
of Israel, as a sign of Your particular favor. In the New Law
we find frequent references to spiritual fecundity: "By their
fruits you shall know them ... Do men gather grapes of thorns
or figs of thistles" (Matt. 7: 16, 20)? But the vine in the New
Testament is used as a symbol of Your Mystical Body (John
15: 1-5). We, the branches, Your members, are to produce
fruits of virtue through our vital union with You.

Those who practice union with You ... and are fertile in
virtue ... enjoy great interior peace, symbolized by the olive.
Strangely enough, that virtue and that peace may sometimes
entail the sufferings and the sacrifice not unlike those which
You, O Prince of peace, began to endure in the Garden of
Olives.

Behold, thus is the man blessed who fears the Lord.

Behold the vision of domestic tranquility and peace which the inspired writer pictures for us! O Lord, bless the families of those united to You in the sacramental state of matrimony! If we are faithful to You, O Lord, and serve You with salutary fear, we too shall enjoy the spiritual fruits of lives wholly consecrated to You.

The Lord bless thee from Sion: mayst thou see the prosperity of Jerusalem all the days of thy life.

O Lord, we humbly beg You to grant Your special graces and blessings to those who dedicate their lives to Your worship and Your holy will! Grant them not only all the graces of ardent members of Your Church on earth, but also the gift of final perseverance and the revelation of Your divine beauty and infinite love in the state of everlasting happiness!

Mayst thou see thy children's children. Peace be upon Israel!

As the children of Israel rejoiced in their numerous population, indicative of their power, may the members of Your holy Church rejoice, too, in the continual spread of Your kingdom on earth and the salvation of souls who have found peace at last through the gift of the true faith.

Glory be to the Father.

Glory be to the Father, Who personally creates and preserves each individual soul! Glory be to the Son, Who has redeemed each individual soul through His intense personal love and concern! Glory be to the Holy Ghost, Who inspires and personally guides each individual soul towards its eternal destiny! May the Father, Son, and Holy Ghost, Who were in the beginning, are now, and ever shall be infinitely good, all-perfect and all-lovable, keep us safe . . . that we may render glory to them for all eternity! Amen.

ANTIPHON: *Behold, Mary has borne us the Savior, Whom John seeing, exclaimed, saying: Behold the Lamb of God; behold Him Who takes away the sins of the world.*

May our zeal be enkindled by the contemplation of this holy mystery of the Incarnation. Beholding with Saint John the spotless Lamb . . . may we be inspired to follow Him closely and, by the purity of our lives, be privileged to share in His perfect oblation.

LITTLE CHAPTER
(Ecclesiasticus 24: 19-20)

*I*N *the streets I gave forth a sweet fragrance like cinnamon and aromatic balm. I yielded a sweetness of odor like the choicest myrrh.*

May the Spirit of wisdom ... exuding the fragrance of virtue through the Nativity scene ... direct us to closer imitation of our divine Lord, by the renunciation of worldly pleasures and the multiplication of acts of love and sacrifice.

VIII

VESPERS

𝒜 T the vespers
of our lives, we continue to praise the Lord ... not now, perhaps, with the exuberant energies of our youth ... but with
the mature and efficient skill and serenity of the professional
expert.

ANTIPHON: *While the King was ...*

Dear Blessed Mother, Queen of heaven, teach us to realize
that although our divine Lord appears to be at rest sometimes,
not interfering visibly with the progress of human lives, or
with the course of events in time, He is always deeply inter-
ested in our every effort to cultivate holiness, to appreciate
spiritual values, and to please Him in every possible way!

PSALM 109

𝒯HE *Lord said to my Lord: "Sit at My right hand till I make
Thine enemies Thy footstool."*

Faith is a kind of television set of the spirit ... equipped to
record divine impressions. Undoubtedly, King David had a set
valuable in quality, since he was so successful in getting a direct
channel from heaven. In this verse the Psalmist, inspired by
the Holy Ghost, sings of the might and majesty of the Messiah,
as he describes for us the invitation given the Son of God to

sit at the right hand of God, the Father almighty. He demonstrates clearly that Christ, the Son of God and our King, holds not simply a title of honor, but a position of royal authority and omnipotent power. Those who deliberately dare to oppose His law are destined for everlasting ruin. Even the enemies of divine Goodness . . . even the evil forces arrayed against the Lord . . . contribute unwittingly or unwillingly to His greater glory. Shortly after His expression of the sublime law of charity, our Lord Himself quotes these words of David the prophet, to confound the scribes and Pharisees (Cf. Matt. 22: 41, 45; Mark 12: 36; Luke 20: 41, 42).

The scepter of Thy power the Lord will stretch forth from Sion: "Rule in the midst of Thine enemies."

Truly, O Jesus, the eternal Father has extended Your spiritual dominion over human hearts, from the time of the first awakening of the chosen people to a belief in the one, true God. Your kingdom, which is not of this world, must and will be extended. You must rule in the midst of Your enemies, as You ruled during the darkest days of Your Passion and Death . . . through the conquest of infinite love.

"Thine is princely power in the day of Thy birth, in holy splendor; before the daystar, like the dew, I have begotten Thee."

O Jesus, Light of the world! Eternal Day, generated by uncreated Light before the command, "Let there be light" (Gen. 1: 3). Essence of holiness, whence all holy men and women receive the light and goodness reflected in their lives! Grant to us, struggling in this dark and dreary world, Your light and Your strength, that we who receive You, the Word . . . may believe in Your name and be ever conscious that we, the children of light, are born "not of blood, nor of the will of flesh, nor of the will of man, but of God" (John 1:13).

The Lord has sworn, and He will not repent: "Thou art a priest forever, according to the order of Melchisedech."

O Jesus, we have the absolute guarantee, not of fickle men, but of eternal Truth, that You are more than the King of all creation Who bequeaths to us a royal inheritance. You are the everlasting Mediator between humanity and divinity . . . the innocent Victim of love offered once in a bloody sacrifice, perpetually renewed in a mystic manner for the benefit and solace of all mankind.

The Lord is at Thy right hand; He will crush kings on the day of His wrath.

Omnipotent Lord! You are an innocent, humble, gentle Saviour, but Your anger is enkindled against those exalting themselves with pride and usurping Your right to rule. Judgment Day will bring about the reward of the good and the punishment of the wicked. Why should we be disturbed, then, about those who ambitiously usurp power? Why should we be troubled about the narrow, selfish conduct and cruelty of those in high positions? You, the just Judge, will mete out justice to every man on the Last Day, according to his works . . . for when men die, "their works follow them" (Apoc. 14: 13). Hence, our chief concern should be to remain in the state of grace . . . and increase our incorruptible treasury of good works.

He will do judgment on the nations, heaping up corpses; He will crush heads over the wide earth.

Nations and peoples have spent many valuable years bickering over the settlement of their political rights and claims . . . their economic advantages . . . their social prestige and positions. Rarely are they concerned about the genuine spiritual welfare of their citizens. What will material power amount to on Judgment Day? O Lord, You are truly the Judge of all peoples! You will reward those who have suffered for Your sake; yet, You will permit not only the corporal destruction but the spiritual ruin of those opposing Your infinite Goodness. Grant that offenders against Your justice may use their time profitably to make amends . . . save their souls . . . in a positive manner minister to Your glory! Grant that through the daily practice of mortification and charity all Christians may ultimately win the favor of eternal spiritual preservation.

From the brook by the wayside He will drink; therefore will He lift up His head.

You have suffered the torrent of abuse, humiliations, physical sufferings, O Jesus . . . not only to redeem us, but to give us Your heroic example to be imitated! Therefore, You lift up Your head among us . . . not as some remote ideal, impossible to be followed, but as a strong, intimate Friend, Who will help us to rise even though we stumble or fall along the way of the Cross!

Glory be to the Father.

Glory be to the Father, Source of eternal goodness and truth! Glory be to the Son, the Word, Who sits at Your right hand, bearing witness of eternal goodness and truth! Glory be to the eternal Spirit of goodness and truth, uniting You, Father and Son, in the infinite love of perfect goodness and truth! As it was in the beginning, is now, and ever shall be ... may the righteous claims of eternal Justice be forever satisfied.

ANTIPHON: *While the King was reposing, my spikenard yielded the odor of sweetness.*

O Mary, Mystical rose, breathing a fragrance of virtue pleasing to the King ... pray that all souls in the care of Holy Mother Church may increase daily in sanctity and in virtues pleasing to the divine Majesty!

ANTIPHON: *His left hand ...*

Although we, Your children, O Lord, are not always mindful of Your loving providence, if You were to withdraw Your sustaining hand for a moment from our support, we would fall back into the nothingness whence we have issued by Your creative power.

PSALM 112

*P*RAISE, *ye servants of the Lord, praise the name of the Lord.*

Youngsters seem to exert so much energy at play. Adults exert so much energy in their various business, industrial, social, political, and recreational pursuits. O you favored servants of the Lord, let not the children of this worldly generation be wiser than the children of light! Exert your spiritual energies ... exercise all your ingenuity ... utilize all your resources ... organize all your efforts ... to praise the name of the Lord!

Blessed be the name of the Lord both now and forever.

Do not wait for Sunday to praise the Lord! Do not wait until some respite from activities gives you the opportunity for formal prayer! Even a very brief consideration of God's goodness will make you desire to praise Him daily ... hourly ... every moment ... in all your thoughts, words and acts ... in all the passing pleasures of time ... in all the timeless joys of eternity.

From the rising to the setting of the sun is the name of the Lord to be praised.

Contemplation of the marvels of Your creation will intensify our desire to know You more intimately and love You more generously, O God, the Creator Whom we adore. Scientists contemplating the wonders of Your creation, O Lord, should lead the chorus of Your praise. Scholars pondering the truth and wisdom of Your creation should live to promote Your glory. All witnesses of beauty or goodness in creation should worship You, its uncreated Cause, by articulate praise and a constant striving for holiness.

High above all nations is the Lord; above the heavens is His glory.

We are over-awed somewhat by the rulers of nations and the dominions held under their sway. We conjecture about the possibility of life on other planets and the wondrous adventure of travelling to Mars. But, O Lord, You have power above all nations ... over all planets and their movements ... and Your glory is far above the heavens which You have created. It would take a man of great genius to arrange a trip to Mars, but You enable the ordinary man of prayer to reach You in spiritual realms beyond Mars.

Who is like the Lord, our God, Who is enthroned on high and looks upon the heavens and the earth below?

Certainly, no merely human being can compare with You, Lord, in power and strength, or virtue, or in the personal concern for the individual souls dependent on You. When we meet renowned executives, authors, rulers, statesmen, diplomats, learned professional men and women, leaders and geniuses in any field ... we admire their intelligence and achievement. Nevertheless, the most brilliant achievements are so infinitesimal compared to Your creation, O infinite Power and Wisdom and Goodness! Strangely enough, too, we

feel more comfortable in conversing with You than we do in
the company of human genius, because we realize that, in spite
of Your wisdom and power and goodness, You have a sympathetic interest in us and in our personal problems.

*He raises up the lowly from the dust; from the dunghill He
lifts up the poor.*

Like the Father You are, O Lord, You support us in all our
needs, desires, and difficulties ... showing Your special love and
sympathy for those in troubled circumstances ... and for those
in physical, or financial, or spiritual distress.

*To seat them with princes, with the princes of His own
people.*

Through the gift of faith we become Your children, O God
... we are raised to the royalty of the Kingdom of heaven.
You often raise meek and humble souls to a high state of perfection ... appointing them as bishops or rulers of Your
Church and, thus, princes of Your people. Of course, all Your
children ... even simple, humble laymen ... may likewise be
considered as princes of Your people ... because of the influence they can exert on other souls less favored ... because they
are endowed with the gift of sanctifying grace, the insignia
of divine royalty ... and because they enjoy such intimate
friendship with You, O King of kings!

*He establishes in her home the barren wife as the joyful
mother of children.*

O Creator of life, You have control over life. You can
render fruitful even our barren endeavors. We pray You to
bless those united in Christian marriage. We pray You and
we rely on You to make every thought, word and action bear
abundant fruit, and result in Your manifold praise. We pray,
too, that You will inspire many noble souls to renounce the
pleasures of the flesh and consecrate their lives entirely to
Your glory ... that their union with You, though barren of
worldly delights, may be rich in eternal blessings.

Glory be to the Father.

Glory be to the Father, Who has created us primarily for
His glory! Glory be to the Son, Who has bestowed on us the
means to attain His glory! Glory be to the Holy Ghost, Who
inspires us to carry the Cross for God's glory! As it was in
the beginning, is now, and ever shall be, may the Lord be

praised, loved, adored, and glorified ... according to the maximum capacity of His creatures, aided by the infinite assistance of each member of the most holy Trinity!

ANTIPHON: *His left hand is under my head, and His right hand shall embrace me.*

O Mary, beloved of God, privileged in your immaculate purity to enjoy the embraces of your divine Son ... pray that an increasing purity of love may draw us ever closer to His Sacred Heart and to intimate union with Him.

ANTIPHON: *I am black ...*

I am black ... yet not so black that the saving grace of the Lord cannot wash away my sins. The sterling quality of a soul is so much more important than the external pigment of the skin. O Mary, Queen of peace, do not allow me to be intolerant and mean and prejudiced ... to judge people merely by their actions, when only God can discern their motives ... to condemn others for irritating habits, when the Lord Himself undoubtedly loves them for their many hidden virtues.

PSALM 121[1]

ANTIPHON: *I am black but beautiful, O daughters of Jerusalem; therefore the King has loved me and brought me into His chamber.*

O daughters of Jerusalem, expectantly awaiting the Messiah for so long! Well may you wonder at this poor human nature ... darkened with the dust of sin ... charred with the smouldering of selfish passions ... suddenly transformed through a Jewish maiden's *fiat* ... exalted finally to the supernatural splendor and dignity of sharing the life and the love of the Lord!

---

1 See page 116.

ANTIPHON: *Now is the winter past.*

In Spring come gladness and hope, with a renewal of life.
Reawaken energy in our sluggish spirits, O Lord, that we may
love and serve You with increased joy and vigor!

PSALM 126[1]

ANTIPHON: *Winter is now past, the rain is over and gone;
arise, my beloved, and come.*

In the warmth and sunshine of Spring, new life germinates,
flowers, and fructifies. In the grace and sunshine of Your
love, O Lord, may souls die to themselves and the world, to
bring forth the fragrant flowers and solid fruits of sanctity.

ANTIPHON: *Thou art become beautiful . . .*

O Virgin most venerable! Through divine favor you have
been made the fairest of women! Obtain by your intercessory
power that we may seek beyond the attraction of earthly delights to the joys inspired by eternal Beauty!

PSALM 147

GLORIFY *the Lord, O Jerusalem; praise thy God, O Sion.*

O, all you who by faith belong to the city of God . . . profit
by this opportunity to praise the Lord! Yes, we may have
many other tasks for which we should like to steal this time.
Let us neglect not this duty . . . this privilege . . . this grace
accorded to us . . . of praising the Lord. Many souls in other
circumstances wish they had this opportunity. Many souls in
concentration camps wish they could be released just an hour
to participate in the formal worship of God.

---

1 See page 128.

For He has strengthened the bars of thy gates, He has blessed thy children within thee.

O city of the faithful ... rejoice in the security which the Lord provides for our welfare! Know that the commands and restraints imposed by God and His Church are calculated by His grace to render us spiritually safe. We, your inhabitants, need never be molested by external assaults, since we enjoy the blessing of the Lord.

He has granted peace in thy borders; with the best of wheat he fills thee.

O you who seek happiness ... strive to grow in the spirit of faith ... pray daily for an increase of faith! The Lord grants to souls of deep faith the fruits of interior peace. He nourishes their life with the best of wheat ... transformed into the living bread of the Prince of peace! O Holy Spirit, grant us the gift of Your heavenly wisdom ... that we may relish more and more the "best of wheat". ... the divine sustenance of our souls. Through Your wisdom, may we relish more and more the lesson taught by our Lord about wheat ... which, to produce fruit, must die.

He sends forth His command to the earth; swiftly runs His word!

O Wisdom incarnate, You have come to earth to teach divine truth to Your people. We are eager to learn more of Your truth! Your Gospel is preached in all parts of the globe. Let us preach it wherever we are, by our conduct! O Holy Spirit of truth, Who abides with the Church and inspires and guides her faithful members, we invoke Your blessing and pray You to bestow on us the gifts of understanding more thoroughly and appreciating more fully the sublime truths of the holy Gospel.

He spreads snow like wool; frost He strews like ashes.

Let us behold all nature through eyes of faith: Striking examples of Your wondrous power, O Lord, may be seen in the snowstorms, when all nature is slowly transformed into white ... or in the sudden bursting forth of the sun, dispelling the haze and fog ... or melting the morning frost. More wonderful still is the power exercised by You, O Lord, in illuminating souls by Your grace ... removing their doubts and fears ... or restoring souls to purity, when they have lapsed into the dull, dreary ways of sin. O Holy Spirit, Who indicates to us such striking manifestations of divine beneficence,

illumine our minds with the gift of counsel, that we may attain
perfect serenity and poise in our religious lives and assist others
by our example to attain that same spiritual peace and
equanimity.

*He scatters His hail like crumbs; before His cold the waters
freeze.*

Let us perceive in all experience symbols of our faith: Another wondrous transformation You effect in nature, O Lord,
appears in pellets of hail. Such storms are symbols of the blasts
in life that test one's courage and stability of soul. Severe and
continued cold also suggests separation from You, through the
cooling ardor of our affection. This is a state intolerable to
the faithful. It is undoubtedly the most bitter pain of the
damned. O Holy Spirit, we beseech You to endow us with
Your gift of fortitude ... that we may emerge triumphant
through all the storms of life with more solid faith, more rug-
ged hope and more ardent charity!

*He sends His word and melts them; He lets His breeze blow
and the waters run.*

Be assured, O faithful followers of God ... no matter how
severe the storm ... no matter how disturbing the experiences
of life ... the Lord omnipotent can cancel their effects by His
simple command. His Spirit shall breathe and melt the hostile
elements ... physical, mental, or moral ... and cause us to be
happy again by a sudden influx of His illuminating grace. O
Holy Spirit, infuse into our minds that heavenly knowledge
which will make us perceive the hand of Divine Providence
in all the major events and all the minor details of our lives.

*He has proclaimed His word to Jacob, His statutes and His
ordinances to Israel.*

O God of Israel! You have favored Jacob and his descendants
with the gift of faith in You. You have granted to the Hebrews
a firm belief in the power of Your justice and judgments. You
have endowed us, the followers of Christ, Your Son, with the
abundant graces and blessings of the Redemption. Grant us,
O Holy Spirit, the gift of piety ... that, loyal to all the divine
commands through the many trials of life, we may cling
courageously and certainly to the faith that is our glorious
heritage!

He has not done thus for any other nation; His ordinances He has not made known to them.

We realize, O God, that the gift of faith is not enjoyed by all, nor in the same degree. May we esteem it gratefully, therefore, and pray daily for its increase. We wish to know You better and trust You more and love You more, O divine Creator! We desire to pray daily, too, for the spread of the faith and we shall endeavor to lead others to it by our example. We pray for the deepening of faith in all who have already received the gift of Baptism. O Holy Spirit, bestow upon us Your holy gift of Fear of the Lord ... that we may recognize the responsibility that is ours as followers of Christ ... that we may be afraid to do anything that will lessen the love and the favor we enjoy as His followers and friends.

Glory be to the Father.

Glory be to the Father, Who has created us as children of faith! Glory be to the Son, Who has so gloriously fulfilled the hope engendered by the faith of the ancients! Glory be to the Holy Ghost, Who infuses into our souls an increase of faith and of hope and inspires us to a love that will help us attain our sanctification! As it was in the beginning, is now and ever shall be, may the Most Holy Trinity be rendered everlasting glory!

ANTIPHON: *Thou art become beautiful and sweet in thy delights, O holy Mother of God.*

O Virgin most venerable! Through divine favor you were created as the fairest among women! Nevertheless, you did not bask self-complacently in this exquisite beauty. Your own deliberate decision to do the divine will revealed your most cherished delight ... radiated the splendor of your transcendent beauty of soul! This is why we revere you as our model, O holy Mother of God!

LITTLE CHAPTER
(Ecclesiasticus 24: 14)

From the beginning and before the world was I created, and unto the world to come I shall not cease to be, and in the holy dwelling place I have ministered before Him.

O divine Wisdom! You are the most admirable of all the perfections of God... coextensive with His existence and inexhaustible source of His love! O Holy Spirit of Wisdom, Spirit of Light and of Love, Whose abiding presence guides and directs the Church in supernatural matters... inspire us with Your wisdom and cultivate in us the spirit of serving You well on earth and ministering to Your glory forever in heaven!

HYMN[1]

Ave, Star of ocean,
Child divine who barest,
Mother, ever Virgin,
Heaven's portal fairest.

Hail, Mary, Star of the sea! You are for us a guiding star amidst life's stormy voyage... transmitting rays of divine Love to all who contemplate the beauty of the heavens. How fittingly are you compared to a star, as Saint Bernard remarks: "Neither does the beam lessen the brightness of the star, nor the Son the inviolateness of the Virgin" (*Roman Breviary*, Lesson 4, September 12). Truly, O Virgin Mother, you are the Gate of heaven, since our salvation came through you and our entrance into heaven can be aided mightily by your intercession!

Taking that sweet Ave
Erst by Gabriel spoken,
Eva's name reversing,
Be of peace the token.

O blessed Lady! The word *Ave*, with which the Angel Gabriel saluted you, suggests to the poetic mind[2] the great contrast between Eva, the first woman, and you, the glorious

---

1 Translation of J. Althestan Riley. Reprinted from *The English Hymnal* (Copyright, London, 1906) by permission of the Oxford University Press.

2 Not poets alone but the early Fathers of the Church, from the second century on, designated Mary as the new Eve. Cf. *Munificentissimus Deus* of His Holiness, Pope Pius XII, issued Nov. 1, 1950, translated into English by Rev. Joseph C. Fenton (Washington, N.C.W.C., 1950), p. 16, par. 39; cf. also *Ineffabilis Deus* of Pope Pius IX, p. 13.

instrument of our salvation . . . between her disobedience to God's command and your submission to the heavenly message . . . between the consequent punishment due to sin and everlasting peace, the reward of fidelity.

> *Break the sinners' fetters,*
> *Light to blind restoring,*
> *All our ills dispelling,*
> *Every boon imploring.*

Our Lady, Refuge of sinners, pray for those enmeshed in the chains of vice . . . hardened by the flinty crust of bad habits . . . blinded by jaundiced, selfish, and slothful desires. Pray for us, that we may see the light of God's grace and correspond to its quickening influence.

> *Show thyself a Mother*
> *In thy supplication;*
> *He will hear who chose thee*
> *At His Incarnation.*

Surely we can rely on your intercession, O Mary, since a mother such as you will always seek to help her children and your divine Son will never refuse your request.

> *Maid all maids excelling,*
> *Passing meek and lowly,*
> *Win for sinners pardon,*
> *Make us chaste and holy.*

Dear blessed Mother! We desire many favors through your intercession, but we seek earnestly for the grace to imitate you in the special virtues characteristic of all your conduct . . . the virtues of humility and purity . . . so pleasing to the Lord!

> *As we onward journey*
> *Aid our weak endeavor,*
> *Till we gaze on Jesus*
> *And rejoice forever.*

With these two virtues as the foundation of our spiritual life, our Lady . . . we desire your assistance, as we strive valiantly to pursue the path of holiness . . . until we finally arrive at the reward promised by our Lord to the "meek," to the "poor in spirit," to the "pure of heart," and to "those who hunger and thirst for justice's sake" (Matt. 5: 4, ff.).

> *Father, Son, and Spirit,*
> *Three in One confessing,*
> *Give we equal glory*
> *Equal praise and blessing.*

Guide us, our Lady, to the joy and blessing of contemplating forever the Beatific Vision . . . that we may praise, love, adore, and glorify our Creator, Redeemer, and Sanctifier, in the sublime mystery of the Unity and Trinity of God! Amen.

VERSICLE: *Grace is poured forth on thy lips.* RESPONSE: *Therefore God has blessed thee forever.*

As we repeat this verse of the forty-fourth Psalm . . . a nuptial song, praising the Messiah King, describing the close union between bridegroom and bride, and illustrating the close relationship which exists between the soul and God . . . we may apply the words also to you, O Mary . . . for you were addressed by the Angel as "full of grace." Surely the Lord has blessed you forever!

ANTIPHON: *O Blessed Mother.*

O blessed Mother of God and channel of His precious graces to us, pray that we may correspond more and more generously with the divine gifts bestowed on us . . . that we may be gracious and willing instruments of God's mercy to others.

*M*Y *soul magnifies the Lord . . .*

This exultant expression of gratitude and praise springs from the profound love of Mary's heart. Not in any stereotyped speech pattern, therefore, does her radiant spirit hymn her joy to You, O Lord . . . but in the simple, original terms which reveal something of the altitude of her interior holiness. Help me, O blessed Mother, to study your spontaneous prayer of praise . . . to discover how best to offer prayers pleasing to the divine Majesty.

My soul magnifies the Lord . . . How can that be? It almost appears to be presumptuous, except that the words were first uttered by you, O blessed Lady, model of humility. I ponder . . . How can my soul magnify You, my Lord? I . . . so insignificant . . . can I magnify You, Lord, the almighty One? There come to me then the words of another great model of humility, Saint John the Baptist, who said, "He must increase; I must decrease" (John 3: 30). Yes, Lord, my soul . . . which is ever bent on magnifying this *ego* . . . must give greater time and attention to You and Your will! My soul must have more room for You and less room for my own selfish whims and fancies. An appreciation of true spiritual values will make me test every action by the query, Is this what *God* wants, or what *I* want? Of course, my soul magnifies You, dear Lord, in theory. Does it magnify You in fact . . . through loving resignation to Your holy will? O dear blessed Mother, help me by innumerable *fiats* today to magnify the Lord . . . that He may continually abide as the welcome Guest of my soul!

And my spirit rejoices in God my Savior.

Mary's supreme happiness arose from her keen appreciation of the highest spiritual favors. When I consider the innumerable special favors You have bestowed on me in life, O God . . . creation, life itself, faith, the benefits of the sacraments, of health, intellectual and emotional joys, the happiness and satisfaction gained from my family and friends, scholarly advantages, my vocation, my profession, manifold spiritual blessings . . . my soul is compelled with Mary to rejoice in You, O God, my Creator, Preserver and Redeemer, to Whom I owe everlasting gratitude and loving service! Teach me, Mary, to strive always for the joys that are eternal!

Because He has regarded the lowliness of His handmaid, for behold, henceforth all generations shall call me blessed.

We have so many career women these days . . . it is interesting, dear Lord, to observe Mary's idea of a career: She simply aspired to be Your humble handmaid. Yet, she had the greatest career ever possible to any woman. Her prophetic statement is indeed verified, for all generations call her blessed. Our Lady realized that You blessed her because of her humility . . . and that all succeeding generations would bless her for the very same reason, as well as for her high privilege of being the Mother of God. But why, O divine Majesty, have You deigned to bestow innumerable favors on ordinary souls . . . on mine, for example? Because, O God, being all-wise and all-good, You know how weak a mortal I am without every favorable influence in my environment. You know better than anyone else the lowliness of the character You have chosen to follow You. Your greatness, therefore, is really more apparent in contrast to my pusillanimity of soul . . . my cowardice . . . my fickleness. Surely, all people who could look at the record of my interior life would realize that You have been magnificently generous in Your bestowal of spiritual blessings, in contrast to my niggardly offerings . . . magnanimously indulgent in Your forgiveness of my numerous and serious betrayals.

Because He Who is mighty has done great things for me, and holy is His name.

Pondering on the divine attributes causes me to admire and revere You, God, *objectively*, as the Essence of absolute perfection. Reflecting on the signal grace granted to our blessed Mother, I am moved to express sentiments of love and gratitude. Reviewing Your consideration for me individually and Your indulgence of my weak human nature, I am stirred to love You *personally*, as my Father and most intimate Friend. Not merely because You are mighty, do I admire You, Lord, but because, being mighty, You have done such great things to me, Your most ordinary creature. And holy is Your name . . . that is, Your name is sacred to me, O Lord, for its power raised me to the supernatural life, wherein I may reach eternal spiritual security and happiness.

And His mercy is from generation to generation toward those who fear Him.

Not only to our Blessed Lady, O Father, have You shown Your mercy, by making her the Mother of the Word incarnate, but to countless generations of the faithful who are privileged to receive the Word incarnate in the Holy Eucharist. We benefit daily by Your mercy, O Jesus, in the abundant satisfaction of our physical, mental, moral and spiritual needs. We benefit especially by Your divine Presence in the Blessed Sacrament of the altar.

He has shown might with His arm; He has scattered the proud in the conceit of their heart.

Not through weak indulgence, do You show Your mercy, O God . . . since You exercise Your majestic might so frequently in the beauty and grandeur of natural phenomena . . . in the display of their ominous power. In the moral sphere, You triumph in invisible victories in Your unceasing combat for souls. You scatter the false strength of those proud souls who mistakenly think they are mighty, although their strength does not reach beyond the physical order.

He has put down the mighty from their thrones and has exalted the lowly.

Aggressiveness is a worldly virtue, O God, but Your preference is for the humility of Mary. You cast down from positions of honor and power the ambitious and selfish and proud . . . all those who seek only themselves and their own comfort. You exalt the humble and lend Your divine assistance to the weak and to those who know that they need You. We admire Your patience, which allows the proud to remain so long in power: they provide opportunities for others to progress in sanctity. We bow our heads gratefully that You have not been too severe in punishing our own sins of pride. We are not really courageous enough to ask for opportunities to cultivate the virtue of humility, although we want to be close to You, because You are "meek and humble of heart" (Matt. 11: 29).

The hungry He has filled with good things and the rich He has sent empty away.

To those hungering for eternal Truth, O God, You give the Word made flesh. To those surfeited with worldly desires, You give nothing, for these self-complacent souls do not know enough to profit from Your divine largesse, nor have they any room for You ... ironically enough, *no room* ... even in their barren hearts!

He has given help to Israel His servant, mindful of His mercy.

Many centuries ago, O Lord, You bestowed the true faith on the ancient Hebrews, who worshipped You and were grateful to You for Your favors. They preserved that faith in You and continued to hope in You, in spite of all their sufferings and in spite of the oppression of all foreign political conquerors. Grant that we, who belong to the spiritual Israel through our membership in the true Church established by You, may also serve You loyally and be ever grateful for Your infinite mercy which we can never fully appreciate.

As He promised our fathers, toward Abraham and His descendants forever.

You made a covenant with Abraham and You honored his descendants by allowing the promised Messiah to be born of his people and to bring salvation to the world. Thus, O God, in Your infinite love and mercy, You have fulfilled the promise made to Abraham concerning his numerous progeny (Gen. 17:5, 6). You have fulfilled Your promise of sending a Redeemer. O loving Father, You will fulfill all the promises made through the teaching of Your divine Son, the Word, Who is eternal Truth.

Glory be to the Father.

Glory be to the Father, Whose name should be magnified and praised and adored ... not only by Mary, but by every beneficiary of His abundant grace! Glory be to the Son, the Saviour, Who makes us sharers in His divine life and its transcendent blessings! Glory be to the Holy Ghost, Who keeps us ever conscious of our dignity as children of God and our special vocation as children of Mary and chosen Spouses of Christ! As it was in the beginning, when God planned the redemption of mankind ... is now, when He showers upon us its manifold benefits ... and ever shall be, even unto eternity ... may He ever be praised, especially for His mercy!

ANTIPHON: *O Blessed Mother and chaste Virgin, glorious Queen of the world, intercede for us with the Lord.*

O blessed Mother of God, Mary, whose virginal purity inspires in us the desire for greater perfection, make us realize that . . . as adopted children of God, living in the state of grace . . . we, too, are temples of the Lord and sanctuaries of the Holy Ghost! Let us reflect often on this sublime favor. O Mary, always most pleasing to the divine Majesty, show us how to act in a manner most pleasing to our Lord Jesus Christ. Glorious Queen of the world and Mother of mercy, pray for all people on earth. Pray especially for priests. Intercede frequently for your daughters who regard you as their ideal of Christian conduct and religious perfection.

IX

COMPLINE

*C*ONVERT *us, O God, our Saviour.*

RESPONSE: *And avert Thine anger from us.*

Before it is too late ... before our time is gone ... before our life is ended, and we stand with empty hands on the threshold of eternity ... convert us, O Jesus, Who came on earth to save us! Convert us from our sinful habits ... convert us from our very mediocrity ... convert us to a Christlike life and to habits pleasing to You. Seeing us earnestly repentant ... seeing us spiritually energetic ... seeing us sincerely in love with You and determined to imitate You, You will avert Your anger from us and grant us the grace of final perseverance.

PSALM 128

*M*UCH *have they oppressed me from my youth, let Israel say* ...

Scanning the Old Testament, O Lord, we sympathize with Your chosen people! Israel had reason to complain of the sufferings endured throughout her long history. Through bitter persecutions she proved the quality of her faith. The Church, the spiritual Israel, seems destined to suffer likewise a series of persecutions ... persecutions which challenge the purity of her belief. As members of the Church militant, O God, we beg You to grant to modern martyrs the courage and endurance to win many converts to the truth. You, Who know all things, know all the slow, cruel martyrdoms that are suffered without any publicity. In the petty "persecutions" of one's daily toil,

every member of the spiritual Israel has occasions of practicing
his faith in many ways ... through sacrifice ... through patience ... through resignation to unavoidable circumstances ...
or through courtesy to unsympathetic personalities. Help us,
Lord, to meet these tests of our faith as heroic soldiers, instead
of fussing and complaining like weeping infants who have no
conception of the battle to be won.

*Much have they oppressed me from my youth; yet they
have not prevailed against me.*

More significant than the bitter account of the assaults, is
the fact of Israel's triumphant victory over the enemies of her
faith! She was reduced to slavery many times ... she suffered
spiritual as well as physical losses. Yet, she did not remain
a slave to sin, but worshipped You, the one, true God. There
is the secret for us and for all sincere Christians. No matter
how fierce the assault ... no matter how seriously we are
wounded by sin ... help us, O God of Israel, to have the courage
and loyalty and faith to fight valiantly on ... that truth and
goodness may ultimately triumph in our souls!

*Upon my back the plowers plowed; long did they make their
furrows.*

Dear Lord, Holy Mother Church impresses upon me every
Ash Wednesday that I am dust and unto dust will eventually
return (Cf. Gen. 3: 19) ... but the Psalmist here shows the
sad results of this condition: "Upon my back the plowers
plowed; long did they make their furrows." Indeed, it seems
that the spiteful do not wait until I shall return to dust, but
they begin their plowing now! Preserve in me, Lord ... as
You did in Saint Lawrence ... a well-balanced sense of humor,
along with a spirit of faith. Help me to smile the serene smile
of one who has gazed often beyond Your sacred Passion to
the love that it reveals! Let me see that the plowers ... so proud
of their own hard work ... are but instruments preparing the
soil for Your harvest. Let that harvest, O Lord, be consecrated
entirely to You ... along with the plow and the furrows.

Of course, Lord, You promised Your followers that greater
or lesser trials would come to those who strive sincerely to
live the life of faith. Admirable are the heroic souls of our
own day who courageously suffer for You all the modern
implements of farming ... the refined tortures of a scientific
civilization ... and its brainwashing.

But the just Lord has severed the cords of the wicked. May all be put to shame and fall back that hate Sion.

Justice demands that the good be rewarded and that the wicked suffer for their crimes. The Lord, the just Judge, so indulgent towards repentant sinners, will deal harshly with those relentless in persecuting members of His Mystical Body. We need not worry, O Lord, about getting our petty personal revenge. We rely on Your justice ... but we pray for Your infinite mercy: "Father, forgive them, for they know not what they do" (Luke 23: 34).

May they be like grass on the housetops, which withers before it is plucked ...

The striking resemblance of uncharitable souls to grass on the housetops surprises me ... yet, the Psalmist is right. Grass on the tops of houses lacks the rich soil required for deep roots. Exposed to the sun, therefore, it withers before it can be very useful. Similarly, many souls highly favored by You, Lord, lack the deep roots of humility and faith. They rely on superficial reasons for their judgments of others. Consequently, like the grass, they wither ... consumed with the heat of their own hostility towards their fellow men. While the Psalmist here calls for the punishment of his oppressors, O God, he actually points out the inevitable spiritual condition of any creature unwilling to profit by Your illuminating grace. Deliver me, O Lord, from all uncharitable thoughts!

With which the reaper fills not his hand, nor the gatherer of sheaves his arms.

The lesson taught me by the inspired writer becomes perfectly clear, O Lord: a person whose heart is filled with hate leads a life that is wasted ... he offers nothing to Your glory ... he offers nothing for society's benefit ... he has nothing for his own satisfaction ... he will never be able to attain the object for which he was created. Deliver me, O Lord, from all uncharitable deeds!

And those that pass by say not, "The blessing of the Lord be upon you! We bless you in the name of the Lord!"

Deprived of the prayers of human friends ... deprived of Your blessing, O God ... deprived of comfort and charity, faith and hope ... the proud and selfish are doomed to be miserable forever. Deliver me, O Lord, from all uncharitable sins of the tongue. Help me to pray daily for my enemies, as well as for my friends!

Glory be to the Father.

Glory be to the Father, Who endowed me with the gift of faith and is willing to increase and deepen that faith! Glory be to the Son, Who has shown me the value of suffering nobly for the faith! Glory be to the Holy Ghost, Who illuminates my mind that it may judge all things according to faith!

PSALM 129

*O*UT *of the depths I cry to Thee, O Lord; Lord, hear my voice!*

How dare I complain about others who treat me so unkindly, when I have been so ungrateful to You, O Lord! In spite of my declarations of love, my habitual sins and stubborn pride speak for themselves. From the depths of my pitiable state I cry to You, O Lord! I am conscious only of my misery and of Your infinite power and goodness. Please give heed to my voice!

Let Thine ears be attentive to my voice in supplication.

In spite of my indifference, my infidelities, and my willful transgressions of Your law, O Lord, kindly hear me . . . for now I am conscious of the horrible wretchedness of being separated from You. I am acutely conscious of the imminent possibility of being separated from You forever. I repent of my sins and promise You sincere and steadfast loyalty according to my strength.

If Thou, O Lord, markest iniquities, Lord, who can stand?

Now, I thoroughly realize my weakness, O Lord! Although I desire perfection intensely, I cannot presume much on this human strength. When even the angels and saints are not pure in Your sight, Lord, how vile must sin-steeped Christians appear! If I have feared ordinary class examinations, how much more should I tremble at Your final examination, O all-discerning Judge of my soul!

But with Thee is forgiveness, that Thou mayst be revered.

Utter shame and grief would drive me away from Your presence . . . or abject fear would freeze the request on my lips . . . but, dear Lord, You are no ordinary human professor or judge. Knowing Your mercy, I cast myself before You and humbly beg Your forgiveness. I rely on Your law of love to operate in my behalf; nor can I be disappointed ... Your Son daily offers Himself to redeem me and all mankind through His love and to teach us the reverence and worship due to You.

I trust in the Lord; my soul trusts in His word.

Down through the ages, the faithful relied on Your promises of a Redeemer, O God. He came ... the fulfillment of this promise ... in the person of the Word made flesh. Therefore, I can confidently rely on Your word, O eternal Truth. My soul can firmly trust in Your word ... hope tranquilly in the ultimate victory over sin ... hope joyfully in eternal life and intimate union with You.

My soul waits for the Lord more than sentinels wait for the dawn.

The night is so long when it is our duty to stay awake and work until dawn ... when we suffer anxiety, fear, or pain and wait for the dawn ... when we are alone and cannot find comfort except with the dawn. Without the light of Your grace, O God, my soul would suffer the darkest of nights. Eagerly I wait for You and Your eternal day ... more than sentinels wait for the dawn.

More than sentinels wait for the dawn, let Israel wait for the Lord.

The people Israel, waiting thousands of year for Your Son, must have been like sentinels waiting for the dawn, O Lord! Through that long, gloomy period the ancient Hebrews continued to believe and hope in the advent of the Messiah. Few of them lived to see their hope fulfilled through the Incarnation. Our spiritual benefits are greater than those of the ancients, who were Your chosen people, O God! The fulfillment of Israel's hope ... the sacred mystery of Divinity redeeming humanity ... is made effective now at every hour some place on earth, where the Holy Sacrifice of the Mass is being celebrated "from the rising of the sun even to the going down" (Malachias 1: 11).

For with the Lord is kindness and with Him is plenteous redemption.

Overlooking the abominable transgressions of the ancients and the colossal conceit of moderns ... overlooking my personal acts of base ingratitude, O Lord, You have shown mercy to

Your repentant children. As the kindest of Fathers, You forgive us and You bless us munificently.

And He will redeem Israel from all their iniquities.

You have redeemed Israel from the captivity of Satan. You have redeemed us from the slavery of sin. Moreover, You have exalted us to the liberty of Your children. With the infinite treasures of Your grace, we have the opportunity to purchase eternal happiness for the holy souls in Purgatory . . . for ourselves . . . and for our fellow members of society.

Glory be to the Father.

Glory be to the Father, Whose mercy brings us hope amidst the depths of our misery! Glory be to the Son, our Saviour, the personal and everlasting fulfillment of our hope! Glory be to the Holy Ghost, Who inspires us to invest wisely and well our redemptive blessings, with confident hope in their eternal dividends! As it was in the beginning, is now and ever shall be, glory be to the most holy Trinity, object of our hope and Essence of charity!

PSALM 130

O Lord, my heart is not proud, nor are my eyes haughty.

The examination of my conscience leaves me no reason to be proud, Lord . . . nor can my eyes, cast down from shame and embarrassment, gaze aloft, disdaining others because of my imagined superiority.

I busy not myself with great things, nor with things too sublime for me.

I must admit, I want to follow Saint Paul's advice to "seek the things that are above" (Col. 3: 1). But I do not busy myself with measuring what others are doing . . . nor do I disturb myself with ambitious longings, seeking to excel in intellectual or spiritual attainments . . . since You, O Source of wisdom, are sufficient for me!

Nay rather, I have stilled and quieted my soul like a weaned child.

Lord, I know I have been guilty of childish conceit and vanity . . . my soul has been puffed up with petty ambitions and pride . . . but You know well that this was due to my infantile ignorance and spiritual immaturity. My only glory now comes from a confident love of You . . . my only longing is to cling more loyally to You.

Like a weaned child on its mother's lap, so is my soul within me.

Like a very small child, I rest inarticulate but content, in the shelter of Your loving protection . . . neither boasting of my own powers, nor belittling the achievements of others. As the weaned child suffers the separation from its mother, so let my soul feel always the longing and desire for You . . . with no other interest except to remain close to You . . . for what else really matters?

O Israel, hope in the Lord, both now and forever.

May every member of the faithful find the same peace and contentment and serene security with You, O God . . . here on earth and forever in Heaven!

Glory be to the Father.

Glory be to the Father, Who created me and made me a child, dependent on His solicitous care and kindness! Glory be to the Son, Who told His followers to become as little children, if they wished to enter His kingdom! Glory be to the Holy Ghost, Who inspires us to contemplate the divine Child, that we may learn to imitate His virtues! As it was in the beginning, is now, and ever shall be . . . infinite glory to the goodness of the Triune God!

LITTLE CHAPTER
(Ecclesiasticus 24: 24)

I am the mother of fair love, and of fear, and of knowledge, and of holy hope.

O Spirit of Wisdom! You have indeed engendered love ... not the superficial attraction due to sensible qualities, but the penetrating discernment and admiration of spiritual beauty, leading to noble and heroic sacrifice.

O Spirit of Wisdom! You are the cause of reverential fear. We would be embarrassed to have our every word tape-recorded ... our every action televised ... our every thought discovered by a sort of psycho-analytic radar. We are not really cowards then, to fear You, since human science causes us to fear, although it is in no way comparable to divine omniscience. Cultivate in our hearts a salutary fear, so that, pure in conscience, we may adore You with profound reverence.

O Spirit of Wisdom! You have inspired us with the highest knowledge, which comes through the gift of faith. Let us ever be zealous in the spread of this knowledge, as we seek all our happiness in its divine Source.

O Spirit of Wisdom! You are the cause of our holy hope: Although all our evil tendencies and habits are stored against us ... stored in every nerve and tissue and muscle of our being ... grant to all our good thoughts, desires and actions the cumulative spiritual power to support and save us on Judgment Day.

RESPONSE: *Thanks be to God.*

We are grateful to You, O Holy Spirit ... for You are the cause of our holy hope of eternal salvation, since You are the cause of our knowledge of God's infinite love and mercy.

VERSICLE: *Pray for us, O holy Mother of God.* RESPONSE:

That we may be made worthy of the promises of Christ.

O Mary, filled with the grace of the Holy Spirit, the words of divine inspiration well apply to you, as "Mother of fair love, and of fear, and of knowledge, and of holy hope." Seat of wisdom and Mother of mercy, pray for us ... your children

... that, loyally devoted to the Holy Spirit, we may strive perseveringly to be worthy of the glorious promises of Your Son, our Saviour.

ANTIPHON: *We fly to thy patronage.*

To be indifferent about the time and place and manner of my death, is not so hard in theory, O blessed Mother ... but in practice it becomes exceedingly difficult. Help me, O holy Mother of God, who saw your adorable Son die on the Cross for love of me! Help me to live a good life and to have a happy death ... perfectly resigned to the will of divine Providence concerning all the attendant circumstances of my death.

CANTICLE OF SIMEON
(Luke 2: 29-32)

Now Thou dost dismiss Thy servant, O Lord, according to Thy word, in peace ...

O blessed high priest, beholding the Lord after years of expectant longing! O profound faith, perceiving divinity through the veil of our humanity! Simeon, inspired by the wisdom of the Holy Spirit, proclaims his eagerness to die, since his earnest hope has at last been satisfied: the promised Messiah and Saviour has come into the world.

Because my eyes have seen Thy salvation ...

O Lord, I have been privileged to see so much more than Simeon. I have been permitted to share daily in Your redemptive Sacrifice for many, many years. I have received You in Holy Communion daily for a good quarter of a century. I have lived under the same roof with Your sacramental Presence for a long, long time. If, at the completion of this OFFICE, death should suddenly come to me, I hope I shall pronounce as joyfully these sentiments of holy Simeon. Please grant my desire, O Lord ... to be concerned so exclusively with eternal realities that I can readily relinquish the concerns of time.

Which Thou hast provided in the sight of all the peoples.

Not forsaking fallen man, You promised him a Redeemer. You provided for the preservation of hope in this Redeemer. You arranged for the salvation of all men. So, too, indulgent towards me in spite of my frequent moral lapses and intermittent indifference, You magnanimously offer me the means of sanctification. As Your supreme gift, You have prepared for me an eternal dwelling in heaven. (Cf. Preface, Requiem Mass.)

A light of revelation for the Gentiles, and the glory of Thy people Israel.

Faith, the light of truth and harbinger of hope, has led the obedient among Your chosen people to attain their glorious destiny, O Lord. Happily, You have generously endowed the Gentiles also with this precious gift. Thus illumined, the members of the Mystical Body of Christ, wish to expand the influence of their faith.

When I come to die, O Lord, like holy old Simeon, may I look back upon a life of zealous faith and fervent hope... ever conscious, as this high priest was, of the infinite benefits our Saviour has destined for every human being in the world!

Glory be to the Father.

Glory be to the Father, the first and final Cause of my life! Glory be to the Son, the Saviour, Who has paid for my soul the infinite price of eternal life! Glory be to the Holy Spirit, Who directs me to discern and desire with Simeon the divine values in life! As it was in the beginning, is now, and ever shall be, praise, honor, glory, and thanksgiving to the Unity and Trinity of the everlasting Godhead!

ANTIPHON: *We fly to thy patronage, O holy Mother of God; despise not our petitions in our necessities, but ever deliver us from all dangers, O glorious and blessed Virgin.*

O holy Mother of God, and our mother through His adoption, we need your protection in all the trials of life... and in all the dangers that threaten our salvation. Help us, O holy Mother of God, in all our necessities, great and small. Deliver us through your powerful intercession from all the physical and moral evils that surround us! O ever glorious and blessed Virgin Mary, teach us by your inspiration and example to live for the deliberate purpose of glorifying God, through perfect obedience to His most holy will ... that death may at last bring us eternal life and the glorious contemplation of the Beatific Vision.

Lord, have mercy on us. Christ, have mercy on us. Lord, have mercy on us.

In the terms of the ancient Eastern liturgy, we again appeal to You, O members of the most holy Trinity! Show mercy to us, in spite of our weak and stupid blunderings ... in spite of our meager response to the invitations of Your divine grace.

VERSICLE: *O Lord, hear my prayer.* RESPONSE: *And let my cry come unto Thee.*

Hear my prayers, Lord, not only for myself, but for all those whom I should remember in this universal prayer of the Church ... for those who most need prayers ... for those who know not how to pray ... that they may look up to heaven and say with confidence, *Our Father.*

LET US PRAY ...

As we close the *Hour of Compline,* we meditate on Your merciful goodness, O God, Who granted us the sublime gift of sending Your Son into the world for our salvation. We ask that we may find favor with You through the intercession of Mary, the blessed Virgin, and through the merits and prayers of all the saints in heaven.

VERSICLE: *Let us bless the Lord.* RESPONSE: *Thanks be to God.*

Let us bless You, Lord ... always ... at times of formal prayer ... at times of leisure ... and at times of active labors ... as we confidently ask Your final blessing. Thanks be to You, O God ... for the privilege of praying ... and the honor of sharing in Your praises!

BLESSING

*M*AY *the almighty and merciful Lord, Father, Son, and Holy Ghost, bless and preserve us. Amen.*

As each day draws to a close, O Father, Son, and Holy Spirit, we come to You for Your appraisal and approval of all our prayers and labors . . . conscious that even our failure spells success, if sealed with the invincible sign of Your Triune blessing. Amen.

ANTHEM OF THE BLESSED VIRGIN MARY[1]

*Q*UEEN *of Heaven, rejoice, alleluia.*

O Mary, Queen of all the angels and saints! We rejoice with you in expressions of exultant praise, as we sing: Alleluia!

For He Whom thou wast made worthy to bear, alleluia . . .

You have lived with the Lord through His perilous, painful journey, from the first moment of the Incarnation, all the way to the foot of the Cross. You have been privileged to share something of His sacred Passion. Even this privilege of sharing His suffering causes joy to well up in your heart now, as you sing: Alleluia!

Has risen as He said, alleluia.

His victory over earth and earthly powers . . . His conquest over sin and its satanic source . . . His glorious Resurrection from the dead, which won for us our redemption and salvation . . . should provoke perpetual paeans of praise: Alleluia!

Pray for us to God, alleluia.

Pray that we may cultivate the art of prayer and of praise . . . that not our lips alone but every fiber of our being will reflect the sincerity of our hearts and our minds, as we utter: Alleluia!

---

1 *The Little Office of the Blessed Virgin Mary* (N. Y., Pustet, 1953), p. 199. See also Britt, *op. cit.*, p. 67.

VERSICLE: *Rejoice and be glad, O Virgin Mary, alleluia.*

Every thought of the Resurrection should stimulate in all souls on earth and in heaven, exultant, exuberant emotions of joy: Alleluia!

RESPONSE: *For the Lord has risen indeed, alleluia.*

No scientist can explain it . . . no atheist can disprove it. The Resurrection of our Lord from the tomb on Easter Sunday remains the dependable, the glorious fact of our faith. Alleluia!

LET US PRAY . . .

Let our minds think often, our Lord, of Your Resurrection, as our hearts repeatedly sing: Alleluia! Alleluia! Alleluia! For Alleluia means "Praise the Lord!" Alleluia is the jubilant expression of gladness and thanksgiving for our redemption. Alleluia is the exultant and glorious cry of hope evoked by Your Resurrection, O divine Saviour! Alleluia is the everlasting reminder of our own future resurrection . . . our pledge and guarantee of perpetual happiness!

X

SACROSANCTAE

To the most holy and undivided Trinity . . .

With the conclusion of THE LITTLE OFFICE, O most holy and undivided Trinity, Father, Son, and Holy Ghost, we again thank You for the high privilege of joining the glorious company of the angels and saints in offering up prayers to Your praise . . . for the great dignity that is ours in representing the Church in supplication for all the members of the Mystical Body. We are quite conscious, however, of our inadequacy, O God, and we implore Your indulgence for our distractions . . . Your forgiveness for our lassitude and indifference . . . Your mercy for our mistakes and mumbling and our marring of the heavenly harmony.

To the humanity of our crucified Lord Jesus Christ . . .

O eternal Father and Holy Spirit, help us to love and praise Jesus Christ, our Lord, Who suffered in His sacred humanity, that He might exalt us, Your children, through His infinite merits, to a participation in His divinity, since "as many as received Him, to them He gave power to become the sons of God" (John 1: 12).

To the fruitful purity of the most blessed and most glorious Mary ever Virgin . . .

O most blessed Mary, ever virgin, as your devoted children we wish to offer up the recitation of this OFFICE in affectionate homage to your immaculate purity, which reflects in a finite manner the goodness and perfection of the Godhead to Whom you are leading us.

And to the company of all the saints . . .

O illustrious members of the Church triumphant! You form the ideal assembly of United Nations, representing every race and land and people . . . knowing more than narrow national interests . . . working beyond the international scope, by seeking the supra-national purpose of the glory of God and the salvation of every individual soul on the globe. Inspire us with this true spirit of Christian charity, O diplomats of heavenly wisdom! Teach us to praise God, to observe His precepts and to assist our neighbors by our prayers and good deeds.

Let everlasting praise, honor, power, and glory be given by all creatures.

Thus, may every creature . . . animate and inanimate . . . reflect the goodness of God! May every intelligent being offer everlasting praise, honor, and glory to the most holy Trinity, Whom we profoundly adore . . . to our Lord and Redeemer, by Whom, and with Whom, and in Whom we offer up the Holy Sacrifice perpetually renewed . . . to the most fruitful purity of the blessed and glorious Mother of God, bequeathed to us by her Son as our mother and model . . . to the company of all the saints, enjoying the blessed triumph of holiness.

And may we obtain the remission of all our sins . . .

May we obtain the remission of all our sins . . . and indulgence for all indifferent or imperfect work, half-finished, or done with slothful spirit. Let us make amends . . . through genuine sorrow for all our transgressions . . . through steadfast purpose of pursuing perfection . . . through our loyal efforts and humble submission . . . through our fervent participation in liturgical worship.

Through all eternity. Amen.

Though we may fall many times through human weakness, O Lord, grant that we may persevere until death, in the state of sanctifying grace. Amen . . . So be it . . . In other words, we *mean* what we are saying, O Lord, and never were we more in earnest.

VERSICLE: *Blessed is the womb of the Virgin Mary, that bore the Son of the eternal Father.* RESPONSE: *And blessed are the paps that gave suck to Christ our Lord.*

O Lord! Your response to the woman in the crowd of Your followers suddenly emphasizes a striking truth: Our Lady's exalted position as Mother of God ... and all the privileges of God-given grace ... are admirable, of course ... but the determining factor of holiness is the observance of the divine law and submission to Your will. Therefore, let us be conscious of our sublime vocation as Spouses of Christ ... but as we go forth to the duties of our active life, O God, let us praise You by our practical virtues. As we sew ... or cook ... or nurse ... or teach ... or suffer the thousand interruptions administrative works entail ... let us be patient and generous and charitable, seeing the hand of divine Providence directing all our affairs. Let us be united with You, O God, imitating You in Your active life on earth and discerning Your image in those we humbly serve.

Our Father. Hail Mary.

Our Father, to Whose providence and protection we entrust all our needs ... make our prayers of praise and thanksgiving, reparation and supplication, issue forth in generous and noble actions! Hail, Mary, full of grace, pray for our perfect and steady cooperation with grace, up to and including the moment of our death!

Here, Lord, I hesitate to say *Amen,* because *Amen* seems like the ending of a prayer. I want to keep on and on ... adoring You ... and loving You ... and praising You ... throughout the ages of eternal bliss! But reverently, I breathe *Amen,* because *Amen* unites me solidly to You and to Your prayer and sacrifice, O Christ, divine High Priest and Victim, as You raise the Host ... the Chalice ... of salvation, praise, and everlasting glory!